D1569296

Flexibility at Work

Flexibility at Work

Critical Developments in the International Automobile Industry

Edited by

Valeria Pulignano

Paul Stewart

Andy Danford

and

Mike Richardson

First published 2008 by
PALGRAVE MACMILLAN
Houndmills, Basingstoke, Hampshire RG21 6XS and
175 Fifth Avenue, New York, N.Y. 10010
Companies and representatives throughout the world

PALGRAVE MACMILLAN is the global academic imprint of the Palgrave Macmillan division of St. Martin's Press, LLC and of Palgrave Macmillan Ltd. Macmillan® is a registered trademark in the United States, United Kingdom and other countries. Palgrave is a registered trademark in the European Union and other countries.

ISBN 13: 978–1–4039–0041–8   hardback
ISBN 10: 1–4039–0041–8   hardback

This book is printed on paper suitable for recycling and made from fully managed and sustained forest sources. Logging, pulping and manufacturing processes are expected to conform to the environmental regulations of the country of origin.

A catalogue record for this book is available from the British Library.

Library of Congress Cataloging-in-Publication Data

Flexibility at work : critical developments in the international automobile
    industry / Valeria Pulignano ... [et al.].
      p. cm.
    Includes bibliographical references and index.
    ISBN 1–4039–0041–8 (alk. paper)
      1. Automobile industry and trade–Management. 2. Industrial relations.
    3. Automobile industry and trade–Production control. 4. Automobile
    industry workers. I. Pulignano, Valeria, 1968–
    HD9710.A2F59 2008
    629.222068′5–dc22

                                                        2008016420

10   9   8   7   6   5   4   3   2   1
17 16 15 14 13 12 11 10 09 08

Printed and bound in Great Britain by
CPI Antony Rowe, Chippenham and Eastbourne

Contents

v

List of Figures

List of Tables

Notes on the Contributors

Dan Coffey is Senior Lecturer in Economics at Leeds University Business School, where he was until recently Director for all economics-related MA Programmes. His research interests span organisation and operations in manufacturing industries, political economy and industrial sociology. His recent projects include a book on production myths and the world car industry, published as *The Myth of Japanese Efficiency: the World Car Industry in a Globalizing Age* (Edward Elgar, 2006). He publishes in a wide range of journals and is the co-editor (with Carole Thornley) of *Industrial and Labour Market Policy and Performance: Issues and Perspectives* (Routledge, 2003) and (with David Bailey and P.R. Tomlinson) of *Crisis or Recovery in Japan: State and Industrial Economy* (Edward Elgar, 2007). He is active in associations which include the European Network for Industrial Policy (EUNIP).

Richard Cooney works in the Department of Management at Monash University in Australia. His research focuses upon the organisation of work, employee skill formation and the implementation of new production practices. Richard is a specialist in the automotive industry having recently completed a large project for the Ford Motor Company of Australia. He has also recently completed a study of the Australian Vocational Education and Training (VET) system in an international comparative context. Richard is currently editing a book examining trade union involvement in VET policy formation and he is co-convenor of the International Conference on Training, Employability and Employment (CTEE).

Andy Danford is Professor of Employment Relations at the Centre for Employment Studies Research, University of the West of England. He has published books and articles on the subjects of lean production, the high performance workplace and union renewal strategies.

Elaine Marlova V. Francisco is Associate Professor and Researcher of the Labour Studies Program at the University of Rio de Janeiro State (UERJ), Brazil. Her main research interests have been related to the sociology of work, workers organizations at the shopfloor and trade unionism.

Geert Van Hootegem is Professor at the K.U. Leuven, Centre for Sociological Research (CeSO), (Belgium). He conducts research on new production concepts, flexibility, lean production, quality of working life, new technology, socio-technical system design, integral organisational renewal, team based work, the information society and globalisation. He is currently involved in fundamental and applied research projects, such as: EMERGENCE, focusing on plausible relocation movements that were caused by technological factors in the eEconomy (in the service sector); STILE, focusing on Statistics and Indicators on the Labour Market in the eEconomy; Kerosine, about the Knowledge Economy and Regional Strategies for Organisational and Sustainable Innovation; and a project on Spatial Data Infrastructure and Public Sector Innovation. He is a member of the Editorial Board of the academic journal 'Work, Employment and Society'.

Rik Huys is senior researcher at the Higher Institute for Labour Studies (HIVA) at the Katholieke Universiteit of Leuven (Belgium). He attained a PhD in 2000 at the Faculty of Social Sciences of the Katholieke Universiteit Leuven with a dissertation on 'The structure of the division of labour in Belgian car assembly plants'. His research relates to the fields of work organisation, quality of working life and surveys on these issues. He is currently involved in the European research project, WORKS that aims at improving our understanding of the changes taking place in work in the knowledge economy.

Christian Lévesque is a Professor of Industrial Relations, Department of Human Resource Management, at HEC Montréal. His research focuses on union revitalisation, workplace innovation and the social regulation of multinationals. He is Co-director of the Inter-University Center on Globalisation and Work (CRIMT) a research network that seeks to understand the social dynamics of institutions and capabilities building in a global era.

Valeria Pulignano is Professor in Sociology of Labour and Industrial Relations at the Katholieke Universiteit of Leuven (Belgium). She is also an Associate Fellow at the Industrial Relations Research Unit (IRRU) at Warwick University and at the University of West of England (UK). She has been Visiting Professor at the School of Industrial and Labor Relations at Cornell University (USA) and Visiting Research Fellow at the UNICAMP – University of Campinas (Brazil). Her main research field is comparative industrial relations in European and non-European countries. A central aspect of her work concerns systems of worker representation at both European and national levels, labour internationalism, trade unionism, change in work organisation and labour markets. She developed extensive work in the automobile sector in and outside Europe. She is authors of publications in *Industrial Relations Journal*, *Work Employment and Society*, *British Journal of Industrial Relations*, *Economic and Industrial Democracy*.

José Ricardo Ramalho is Professor of Sociology at the Federal University of Rio de Janeiro (UFRJ), Brazil. His main research interests have been related to the sociology of work, trade unions and working class movements, and development studies.

Mike Richardson's research interests include labour history, as well as industrial sociology and the labour process. Recent publications include Richardson, M. (2006) 'Rapprochement and Retribution: The Divergent Experiences of Workers in Two Large Paper and Print Companies in the 1926 General Strike', *Historical Studies in Industrial Relations*, No. 22, 27–52. Together with Andy Danford, Stephanie Tailby, Paul Stewart and Martin Upchurch in 2005 he authored *Partnership and the High Performance Workplace: Work and Employment Relations in the Aerospace Industry* (Palgrave, 2005).

Graham Sewell is professor of organisation studies and human resource management in the Department of Management & Marketing, University of Melbourne, Australia. Prior to this appointment Graham was professor and chair in organisational behaviour at the Tanaka Business School, Imperial College London. From August 2004–July 2005 he was the Spanish Ministry of Science & Education visiting professor at the Universitat Pompeu Fabra,

Barcelona. He has also held visiting appointments at the University of South Florida, the University of California Santa Cruz, and the University of California Berkeley. He gained his PhD in urban planning from Cardiff University in 1994. Graham has been researching teamwork and workplace surveillance since the late 1980s and has published extensively on these topics in journals such as the *Academy of Management Review*, the *Administrative Science Quarterly*, and *Sociology*.

Paul Stewart is Professor of the Sociology of Work and Employment in the Department of HRM at the University of Strathclyde, Glasgow. He has researched and published on the labour process and labour relations in the international automotive industry for many years and is former editor of *Work, Employment and Society*. He is a member of the editorial board of Capital and Class.

Carole Thornley is Senior Lecturer in the School of Economic and Management Studies at the University of Keele, where she is also Director of Postgraduate Research for the Institute for Public Policy and Management. She is an expert on employment systems and structures, industrial organisation and business strategy, and has previously worked for major global manufacturing multinationals in Belgium. She is very widely published in books and journals which include the *British Journal of Industrial Relations*, the *Industrial Relations Journal*, and *Work, Employment and Society*, and has worked on numerous commissioned projects. She is an experienced adviser to trade unions and has submitted evidence to many official inquiries and reviews. She is co-author of a forthcoming book (with Dan Coffey) called *Globalisation and the Varieties of Capitalism Debate*, to be published by Palgrave Macmillan.

Introduction: 'Flexibility' at Work. Critical Developments in the International Automobile Industry

Valeria Pulignano, Paul Stewart, Andy Danford and Mike Richardson

It is sometimes tempting to describe labour and organisational relations in the international automobile industry as having undergone significant transformations in recent years as if there were ever a period of calm in the sector. Workers and researchers of the industry understand well that the sector has always been a hot bed of technological and social change. The ramifications of changes have always spread widely beyond the reach of the sector. This is true whether we consider the early impact of Ford's production philosophy or more recent developments associated initially with so-called 'Japanisation' and the more recent, and associated 'lean production' paradigm. Whether it is education, health or for example, the UK civil service, ideas from the automotive sector have had a controversial impact.[1] Yet in stating this by now fairly well accepted observation we would want also to emphasise the notion that the management of labour relations is arguably, the critical factor drawing the interest of actors from a range of other sectors. More than this, we also want to make the point that the major ideas, which arguably defined the progress of the sector from the standpoint of work and employment relations, have carried significant political and ideological consequences. This is again clear when we recall the ideological nuances of the so-called Japanisation school or the somewhat less well hidden agenda of the lean production paradigm in its many, varied guises, one of which reappears in variants of High Performance Work Organisation literature.

What all lean-inspired contemporary management approaches to labour in the sector have in common is a questionable assumption about the historical origins of sector difficulties, problems around

1

technology accepted and bearing in mind the fact that these too are indelibly tied to questions of the social organisation of work. This is that the critical difficulties in the sector are generated by what Alfred Sloan, General Motors' first Mister Big interpreted as the problem of labour and that if the latest agenda for the management of change is properly implemented the problems of labour, which become the problems of management, will wither away. In some respects, this lean production view of work is really a modern day version of the old human relations lament for the relative scarcity of the intelligent manager. Except that in the modern guise of lean production, this is for sure a seeming advance on the pre-war human relations conceit that only clever managers, the diligent leaders, could make the incompetent or stupid worker understand the needs of the business. This new conceit will apparently allow the firm to thrive in a strategically sophisticated context where 'thinking-harder-not-working-harder' workers will be involved in 'managing' the production process. Lean production is seen as the latest great ideological avatar of employee involvement, transforming the dull assembly line into a continuously improving (learning?) environment. It is not the workers, in other words, it's the managers, stupid! This is far from parody when one considers some of the eulogies penned for the benefits of lean production, beginning with the *Machine that Changed the World* way back in 1992. Yet why was this inherently misconceived? What have been the most trenchant critiques of this managerial philosophy?

There were two early sources of critique of the certainties of lean production. The first, inspired by the *Labor Notes* current in the US, principally Mike Parker and Jane Slaughter (1988) and later Kim Moody (1997), ran parallel to the developing strategic opposition of the Canadian Auto Workers' (CAW). The CAW in particular, and uniquely, developed a strategic agenda to counter lean production in the automotive industry. Unusually, as a result of its bargaining strength, the CAW was able to conduct a rare study into the impact of lean production on workers and notably at CAMI (Suzuki Motor Corporation and General Motors of Canada. See Rinehart *et al.*, 1997). In Europe, via the Transnational Information Exchange (TIE) and especially in the UK, this work was reflected in the thinking of the Transport and General Workers' Union (See Fisher, and the TIE) and a number of others took up the baton, including Stewart and

Garrahan (1995), and the Autoworkers' Research Network (See Stewart *et al.*, 2008 *forthcoming*). This work focused both on the impact of lean on autoworkers' quality of life at work and the role of management and all in the context of path-dependant, managerial regimes. Their conclusions highlighted the manner in which lean is more than an ideology or a disputed view of the trajectory of the automotive sector (see Coffey's recent critique, 2006 and Chapter below). Whatever we make of the arguments of the protagonists of lean production regarding superior firm performance, one incisive conclusion of the labour movement research has been the extent to which contemporary automotive firms' strategies extend while at the same moment they deepen the intensification and extensification of labour. However we term the new production strategies in the sector, they nevertheless constitute a 'new politics of production' (Stewart and Martinez Lucio, 1998) wherein work is becoming more onerous for all workers. This is seen to be due to the fact that there is a driven quality to the management of labour which seeks to sustain an assault upon carefully developed labour standards originating in the protection of workers. The social and institutional context to this is of course the conflict between capital and labour, usually, though not always, reflected in the trade union histories in various firms.

Research by some members of the Autoworkers' Research Network illustrated the ways in which lean was both distinctive from and continuous of fordist forms of management. In this they took something from Burawoy's view that managerial relations at work represent historically contested forms of hegemony constituted by various forms of 'Factory Regime'. (Stewart *et al.*, 2004). (See amongst other salient labour focused critiques, Graham, 1997; Stephenson, 1996; Danford, 1997; Yates, 1998). This significantly made the point that unions can be and often are powerful players in this contest. The other signally vital point in all this was precisely to draw attention to the relatively limited, or constrained, scope of managerial imperative. Finally, this had the added merit of undermining the socially neutral view of lean production propounded by management. The second source of critique of the lean agenda was provided by Gerpisa.[2] The Gerpisa international research network deserves great credit within the academy for unpicking the 'conceptual deficit' (Charron and Stewart, 2004) of lean production. In highlighting fractured, company-path dependent models of what they term 'Productive Models', Boyer and Freyssenet (2002) demonstrated the social and institutional character of six profit strategies: BMW's 'quality strategy' (see also Volvo in its Uddevalla period – 'Reflective Production'); 'diversity and flexibility' (Wollard before 1945 in the UK, USA and Japan); 'volume strategy' (Volkswagen and Ford, post-1945); 'volume and diversity' (GM); 'permanent reduction in costs' strategy (Toyota – or the so-called lean agenda); finally the Honda approach, which they term, the 'innovation and flexibility' strategy. These depend upon the configuration of three variables – productive organisation, approach to product policy and the nature of the firm's employment relationship.

Our view is that, if we want to critically analyse the form and character of the recent transformations in the international automobile sector, we need to be committed again to a view derived from concrete analysis of particular forms of management-labour relations in the sector in various countries due to particular issues in each geographical, social and political space. Since the 1970s, succeeding profitability crises have impacted ever increasingly upon labour but also we will see not only that labour is far from passive but that the historical trajectory of the company itself lays down the parameters within which workplace social contests occur.

The central objective of this book is to examine the form and character of a number of recent transformations in the international automobile industry by using both national and comparative case analysis. The aim is to assess the extent to which the recent transformations of production and labour organisation achieve forms of flexibility in the international automobile industry distinguishable from so-called lean production. These studies indicate a number of key important developments within the lean paradigm itself, some associated with the HPW principles. Moreover, and unfortunately for those hoping that lean would lead to positive outcomes for most workers in the sector, the evidence here illustrates the extent to which a 'reformed' lean production organisation still generates deleterious outcomes for workers' Quality of Working Life. In particular, the book examines the nature of such recent developments (i.e. outsourcing, modularisation, high performance workplaces, etc.) and their impact on production organisation, the organisation of labour, employee and labour relations, and the quality of working life in the sector worldwide: Italy, United Kingdom, Belgium, France, Mexico, Australia and Brazil.

The book is in two parts. Both parts cover developments in the international automotive industry and the first in particular comprises a rich cross-border comparative analysis. The second part presents in-depth national-based case study analysis covering recent transformations in the car industry in European and non-European countries. Both parts assess the extent to which recent organisational practices illustrating the most radical changes in the sector in the last decade, represent a pattern of organisational phenomenon known as lean production. To what extent do they lead to different forms of social control at work including different forms of labour compliance? What is the impact of trade unions on the inside of these sectoral changes? In our view therefore, the main aim is to critically examine the nature of these developments and their implications for work organisation, the organisation of production, employee relations and the quality of working life. In particular, our central aim has been to assess how far such developments can be regarded as autonomous, company specific transformations, or whether they have been stimulated in their own particular way by the spread of lean production. This is all by way of addressing the extent to which these new developments can be considered as specific and isolated forces in their own right. Each case study involves the examination of the transformation of the production process, its impact on patterns of flexibility at work, employment regulation and labour relations and the form of social control under recent developments in manufacturing. More specifically, the transformations of labour organisations and employment relations, as the main form for achieving flexibility, are taken into account.

Research reported here helps to shed light on two main outcomes. Firstly, the economic rationale of the 'market' regulating inter-firm relationships, combined with productive and organisational regimes of so-called high performance workplaces, emerge as the main factors governing recent labour and employment relations in the international automobile sector. Secondly, the social effects on the workforce and the labour-management relations within the new 'market' regulating workplaces can be located in terms of Burawoy's notion of contested forms of workplace social relations. This context produces new challenges for the trade union movement. In particular, this emphasises the necessity for labour to respond in a coordinated way through enacting power resources locally and internationally.

Simultaneously they must seek to enhance the scope for bargaining at both macro (policy initiatives with the national government) and micro-levels (cross-border plant-level negotiation). We consider this in the context of changes to work organisation, human resource management, the organisation of production, employee relations and quality of working life.

Structure of the book

The book consists of eight chapters, including the introduction.

The first part, 'Developments in the International Car Industry: The Comparative Perspective' consists of three chapters. In Chapter 1, Valeria Pulignano and Paul Stewart highlight the various forms of employment regulation and control in contemporary workplaces characterised by the establishment of new 'multi-enterprise' settings. The central question here is the changing nature of labour control in relation to new patterns of employment and their effects on workplace representation and flexible working practices. The chapter addresses evidence taken from three multi-enterprise organisations in international automotive manufacturing (Fiat-Italy, VW-Brazil and Renault-France). Consideration is given to the idea of an emerging new 'bureaucracy' while exploring the nature of the new patterns of employment regulation and labour control. In Chapter 2 Andy Danford, Mike Richardson, Valeria Pulignano and Paul Stewart present survey data of multifaceted employee experiences of work on the lean production lines of three European car plants. The main research question addresses the employee-centred claim of the original IMVP researchers. This was that lean manufacturing offered something better for workers by contrast with so-called Fordist/Taylorist production systems. This is summed up by the lean production mantra 'working smarter not harder' which reputedly encapsulates a process providing space in which management techniques establish a more participative and less stressful work environment. The data is utilised to explore a number of inter-linked themes concerning the impact of shifts in the labour process and employment relations under lean production regimes. Specifically, a number of assumptions governing the effects of lean manufacturing techniques on employee well-being at the workplace level are challenged. For instance, the utility of new cooperative industrial relations systems, the extent of employee autonomy – and management surveillance – on the car assembly line, and the condition of productive labour on the shop floor measured by such material factors as changes in workload levels, work ergonomics, the intensity and speed of work and reported levels of stress. The chapter highlights a significant gap between the rhetoric of lean production and workers' lived experiences at work. These include limited worker consultation and participation; a lack of employee autonomy and discretion; and a degradation of employment conditions manifested in patterns of labour intensification through conventional means and this also includes problems of managerial surveillance and worker stress. The chapter concludes that when viewed in conjunction with the many critical studies that follow the labour process tradition, our data highlight the shortcomings of the lean production paradigm, underpinned as it is by a 'technologist' conception of history and a position that is consequently neutral in terms of class relations and struggle.

Dan Coffey and Carole Thornley, in Chapter 3, reconsider the myth of lean production through a re-examination of the original MIT data from the late 1980s. The data was held up as evidence of the superior organisational advantages and performance outcomes among Japanese auto manufacturers. According to the MIT protagonists, should Western firms adopt the same techniques and strategies, they could expect lower hours of assembly plant labour required to make cars at any level of factory automation. 'Lean production' – a Western term – was invented and promoted in this connection, giving rise to an enormous subsequent literature, both prescriptive and critical. The practices of one car producer in particular, Toyota, were identified as the key to success by the apostles of lean production. An alternative interpretive reading of the original survey data is first advanced, pointing to quite different conclusions from those promoted by the original MIT researchers. Coffey and Thornley then consider the relevance of this reading for an analysis of labour process concerns. The themes of the chapter are set against the background of industrial crisis which provided the context for the career launch of lean production.

Part II 'Developments in the International Car Industry: The National-based Perspective' consists of four chapters. In Chapter 4 Geert Van Hootegem and Rik Huys discuss the question of the extent to which the automotive assembly industry is still a vital pillar in the Belgian economy. The question is drawn from evidence that the scope for local policy-makers to support the globalised auto industry in Belgium is limited. The authors identify three important competitive factors which influence the decisions on production allocation of models, on production volume and on investments to individual car assembly plants. These relate specifically to working time arrangements, the establishment of an extensive and efficient supplier network and the availability of a qualified workforce. A number of measures are proposed that governments can implement to support the competitive position of local car assembly plants while avoiding mere concession bargaining. This chapter also addresses a number of policy initiatives resulting from a task force on the assembly sector in Belgium aimed at keeping an enduring presence in the region. This task force is a good case upon which to assess the extent to which governments are still able to respond to the pressure exercised by the global economy. A review of the action points resulting from the task force in order to increase the level of competitiveness of local assembly plants shows an emphasis on cost reduction. As such, the action plan is testimony of a defensive 'low road' approach in which the hope is that short-term cost-driven measures will keep activities in the country, or at least slow their delocalisation. As a way out from this short-term cost reduction approach, the chapter advocates broadening innovation funding from technological innovation to innovation on work organisation. In such a 'high road' approach to competitiveness, the emphasis is put on quality and innovation by qualified employees. This enhanced use of human skills and knowledge requires a more holistic approach to the shaping of work tasks and decentralisation of decision-making. The task force action plan however fails to focus on longer-term policy measures to support the enhancement and exchange of knowledge of new forms of work organisation. The predominant low road approach taken by the task force supports the argument that due to globalisation governments must increasingly manage their national economies in such a way as to adapt them to the pressures of trans-national market forces.

In Chapter 5 Richard Cooney and Graham Sewell highlight the diversity of production organisations in the Australian automotive industry, challenging the idea of a global convergence towards a monolithic model of lean production, even in what effectively is a peripheral player in the international automotive industry. In examining recent developments in the Australian automotive industry the chapter outlines two eras of industry reform; an era of state sponsorship of lean production, followed by an era of deregulation and diversification in production organisations. The chapter focuses upon the reintegration of conception and execution within work organisations during the reform process, arguing that different rubrics of rational and normative integration are observable within different firms. The chapter compares the two most divergent cases of production organisation in the Australian industry, those of Ford and Toyota. Ford has developed an organisation of production based upon mass customisation. This organisation of production is allied to forms of work organisation based upon the product flexibility of employees and the normative reintegration of conception and execution. Toyota, on the other hand, has developed an organisation of production based upon lean production and this is allied to a work organisation based upon functional flexibility of employees and the rational reintegration of conception and execution.

The purpose of Chapter 6 is to assess labour relations and working class organisation in lean plants of the auto industry in Brazil. In this chapter José Ricardo Ramalho and Elaine Marlova V. Francisco refer to the case of the VW industrial unit of Resende, in the state of Rio de Janeiro, inaugurated in the mid-1990s, which introduced a new form of organising production, known as the 'modular consortium'. The chapter illustrates that while the production organisation at Resende was presented as an innovative system, certainly when it comes to labour relations the new system of production is very traditional, relying on intensive and cheap labour. On the other hand, it is possible to consider that new dimensions for worker and trade union participation and organisation on the factory floor have developed over the last few years. These are seen as providing elements for a debate about the accumulation of new practices of resistance in restructured plants.

In Chapter 7 Christian Lévesque examines the drive of a multinational firm to achieve higher levels of flexibility in three auto parts plants in Mexico. Over the period of the study, this multidivision MNC shifted from a decentralised to a centralised approach based on a unilateral model of workplace flexibility in which workers and the union were excluded from the decision-making process. The

chapter considers how local actors, managers as well as union representatives, are coping with the pressure from the headquarters to
increase flexibility. Are these actors internalising the requirements of
the new flexible workplaces, adapting it to their own local environments or developing their own approaches? The shift from a decentralised to a centralised approach has met with different kinds of
responses from local actors. They range from compliance to open hostility and opposition. Three distinct patterns of flexibility and workplace relations are described: full flexibility achieved by excluding the
union, numerical flexibility attained through micro-corporatism and
functional flexibility obtained through a contested joint regulatory
process. From these findings the author argues that local managers are
not passive agents who merely implement the policies laid down by
headquarters. They shape the outcome of these policies and formulate
strategies on the basis of their own views of how best to achieve the
firm's objectives. They internalise the requirements of the new flexible
workplaces but adapt them to their own local environment. Local
union representatives can also alter and influence the patterns of flexibility. In order to do so, however, they must develop their power
resources. In workplaces in which the local union is unable to mobilise
its potential external and internal resources, it is by and large simply
excluded from the change process. Overall, this study shows that, even
in a context in which institutional and corporate policies are placing
strong constraints on local actors, workplace regimes have a degree of
relative autonomy and local actors can devise strategies that enable
them to be involved in shaping those regimes. The implementation of
flexibility through the imposition of a unilateral model is based on the
assumption that such a model is more efficient, irrespective of institutional and local arrangements. In two of the cases, this assumption
was challenged and alternative models prevailed. In a context in
which there are competing narratives about the efficiency of workplace regimes, local actors, particularly local unions, must develop
their capacity to frame these narratives.

In conclusion we can make three broad observations. The first is that
in those workplaces where lean production (in terms most obviously
of work organisation) in its various forms is still relevant, the situation
has not improved markedly for the work force and especially in terms
of the quality of working life measured with respect to stress and work
intensification and extensification. This clearly has other ramifications

for labour which is beyond the brief of this book but is nevertheless an avenue for further research for those authors here adopting a Critical Social Relations perspective. While basing analysis on a critical and materialist understanding of workplace change, a CSR approach notably urges caution in the face of a taken-for-granted enthusiasm for new forms of work and employment. The emphasis is rather upon a critical challenge to dominant paradigms derived largely from a managerial view of the latest wisdom for work reorganisation.

Our second conclusion is that in those workplaces where other changes in production reorganisation have occurred (see the modular factory), 'market relations' seems to be the predominant driver of social relations and notably the employment relationship. This is to say that while work organisation is still critical, the defining context is that of internal market politics which increasingly forms the backdrop to the development of HR policy across the sector. In short it has become functional to the new system of domination. Moreover, this is especially important because, as we just pointed out, whatever developments have occurred in lean production on the line, the social effects on the workforce remain corrosive.

Finally, it is obvious that the space in which trade unions can operate has become increasingly more problematic since remaining welded to traditional production politics is insufficient, and has clearly been so for some time past. Paradoxically this does not mean that the traditional fare of trade unionism is less important, rather that the agenda within which this is driven has changed. Our argument is that while issues around workplace bargaining associated with terms and conditions remain highly salient, the new production politics created by the dispensation of lean and the HPWP brings labour immediately into the arena of workplace control bargaining over the nature and impact of work organisation and technological subordination. This new politics of production has thrown in the imperative of engagement with issues beyond the quotidian exclusion of a rough, physically, difficult labour process for the issue of daily work place security is now, indelibly, one of plant survival as the chapter by Geert Van Hootegem and Rik Huys illustrates. Terms and conditions are fought over not only locally, and certainly now this does not even mean at plant level, but rather at the level of state intervention which is obviously, driven by the character of global changes to the automotive sector. Yet, whatever the weaknesses of labour which many commentators, including those writing here have identified, Christian Lévesque highlights the important extent to which labour interventions do make a very substantial difference to outcomes for shop-floor workers.

Notes

1 'How can a Hospital become a "lean Hospital"?' Wherry B and Burnell, 2006 www.focused-on.com. See also the current campaign by the UK government to introduce lean production in the civil service.
2 Group d'Étude et de Recherche Permanent sur l'Industrie et les Salariés de L'Automobile – Permanent Group for the Study of the Automobile Industry and its Employees.

References

Boyer, R. and Freyssenet, M. (2002) The Productive Models: The Conditions of Profitability. Basingstoke: Palgrave Macmillan.
Canadian Auto Workers (1993) *Workplace Issues: Work Reorganisation – Responding to Lean Production.* Willowdale Ontario: CAW Research and Communications Department.
Canadian Auto Workers (1995) *Fight Speed-Up.* Willowdale Ontario: CAW Research and Communications Department.
Charron, E. and Stewart, P. (2004) 'Lean Production – the conceptual deficit' in Charron and Stewart (eds) *Work and Employment Relations in the Automobile Industry.* London: Palgrave Macmillan.
Coffey, D. (2006) The Myth of Japanese Efficiency. The World Car Industry in a Globalising Age. Edward Elgar: Cheltenham.
Danford, A. (1997) 'The "New Industrial Relations" and Class Struggle in the 1990s', *Capital and Class*, no. 61 (Spring) pp. 107–41.
Fisher, J. (1995) 'The Trade union response to HRM in the UK: The Case of the TGWU', *Human Resource Management Journal*, vol. 5, no. 3, pp. 7–23.
Graham, L. (1997) 'On the Line at Suburu', *International Labour Review*.
Moody, K. (1997) *Workers in a Lean World.* London: Verso.
Parker, M. and Slaughter, J. (1988) *Choosing Sides. Unions and the Team Concept.* Boston: South End Press.
Rinehart, J., Huxley, J. and Robertson, D. (1997) *Just Another Car Factory? Lean Production and its Discontents.* Ithaca: ILR Press.
Stewart, P. and Garrahan, P. (1995) 'Employee Responses to New Management Techniques in the Auto Industry', *Work Employment and Society*, vol. 9, no. 3, pp. 517–36.
Stewart, P., Richardson, M., Danford, A., Murphy, K., Richardson, T. and Wass, V. (2008) *'We Sell Our Time No More': Workers' and the Struggle Against Lean Production in the UK Automotive Industry.* London: Pluto Books *(forthcoming).*

Stewart, P. and Martinez Lucio, M. (1998) 'Renewal and Tradition in the New Politics of Production', in Thompson, P. and Warhust, C. *Workplaces of the Future*, Basingstoke: Macmillan.

Stewart, P., Lewchuk, W., Yates, C., Saruta, M. and Danford, A. (2004) 'Patterns of Labour Control and the Erosion of Labour Standards: Towards an International Study of the Quality of Working Life in the Automobile Industry (Canada, Japan and the UK)', in Charron and Stewart (eds).

Stephenson, C. (1996) Uddevalla 'The Different Experience of Trade Unionism in Two Japanese Transplants', in Ackers, P., Smith, C. and Smith, P. *The New Workplace Trade Unionism. Critical Perspectives on Work and Organisation.* London: Routledge.

Transnational Information Exchange (1992) New Management Techniques. TIE/Vauxhall Shops Stewards' Conference. Liverpool, January.

Yates, C. (1998) 'Defining the Fault Lines: New Divisions in the Working Class', *Capital and Class*, 66, Autumn, pp. 119–47.

Womack, J., Jones, D. and Roos, D. (1991) *The Machine that Changed the World.* New York: HarperCollins.

task and responsibility is clearly defined by Fiat. As a result, conventional forms of control, which are employed through the use of team work as a potential tool to discipline employees, operate in conjunction with structured rules for managing employment relationships across the diverse firms where pay is linked to company performance. However, in Italy, this linkage is not 'voluntary' but rather governed by sector-based rules, which it is assumed, ensure regulated flexibility. As a result of the 1993 Social Pact (or tripartite agreement), bargaining assumed a more decentralised pattern at the company level in Italy, but the national industry unions and employers' associations still retain control over the negotiation of employment conditions. Centrally negotiated guidelines are adapted to circumstances at local level so that where company or plant-level bargaining occurs, negotiations produce agreements that do not replace strong industry-wide pattern bargaining. Pay increases (and bonus) – negotiated at company level every four years – have to be linked to the results of the so-called development programmes agreed between management and unions at sector level.

It is important therefore to understand that labour regulation, as a system incorporating penalties and disciplinary rewards, underscores Fiat's monitoring of its suppliers' performance. In this respect the system can be understood as an instrument of governance of the contractual relations between buyer and supplier. Thus, problem-solving within each supplier firm turned out to be an activity driven essentially by fear of penalty or, the acknowledgment of a reward, from Fiat. Flexibility is thereby tied technically to the production process of the entire organisation and is seen as crucial to the achievement of the desired level of assembler:

> At multi-enterprise workplaces flexibility means to co-operate with the interests of the whole organisation. This is achieved by Fiat through assessing the level of performance reached by each supplier, and it is therefore the result of calculative or economic rules, which play in order to govern inter-firm relations (Fiat Production Manager – July, 2000).

These calculative rules notably have a profound impact on employment relations. In particular, contract companies and employees are subject to similar forms of evaluation that prioritise performance-related production incentives. In short, performance-related pay links worker remuneration to enterprise contract. However, as already indicated, the nature of this link is regulated at the company level in accordance with arrangements negotiated with the national union at sector level. Thus, poor annual assessment of firms held responsible for stopping or slowing production is measured along the power relations between the car manufacturer and the suppliers and from there to the employee. As a Fiat employee remarks, the result may be a reduction of individual reward:

> Last week Fiat found out that some of the wheels we sent did not conform to the standard of quality they were expecting. Of course this is not Fiat's responsibility, but it is the responsibility of the supplier responsible of manufacturing the wheels. That supplier is paid for delivering a good product. The worker who produced the faulty wheels was penalised, at the end of the day he lost money he could have earned as individual reward. This would not have happened previously whether the wheels had been produced by Fiat employees since everything would have been accommodated informally (Fiat Employee – June, 2000).

This sets up a dynamic whereby employees' cohesion and commitment is secured by the threat to individual earnings. Workers understand how annual assessments used by multi-enterprise organisations are very much part of the creation of a form of 'consumption' whose rules are shaped by market rationale. As one employee in TNT put it: 'Performance assessment is how management is monitoring the production process. We are assessed internally by the company but on the basis of what Fiat will say about us'.[3]

Contracting out in Renault

Despite a long tradition of vertical integration, the challenges posed by globalisation since the mid-1980s led Renault to broaden the range of products while increasing quality. Restructuring became key in meeting this challenge. In the attempt to reform assembly-line work and production, Renault used the reorganisation model inspired by notions of Japanese total quality management. As Freyssenet (1999a) remarks, a wide-ranging debate developed between management, trade unions and external experts with the aim of outlining the transformations that the company would need to undergo. Among these were changes to the way skill was negotiated, change in the management of working time, reorganisation of work, and development in training and professional orientation. Some new concepts emerged with the diffusion of teamwork, such as the Elementary Work Unit (*Unité Technologique Elémentaire*). Moreover, new principles for contractual relations between suppliers and assembler were introduced which contributed to the expansion of contracting out.

Contracting out grew more substantially over the mid-1990s, involving the use of contractors in both service and production activities operating directly on-site. A particular example of this practice was the Renault truck plant in Sandouville in the north of France, between 1998 and 1999. Here, contracting out mainly consisted in the location of suppliers inside Renault's plant. This resulted in a number of on-line parts assemblies (i.e. door, seat, head liners, fuel tanks, wiring and cabling, carpet, door panels, dash board, console, bumper) and services (i.e. logistics and maintenance) were contracted out to supplier firms. At the beginning of 2000, 621 out of 3,700 employees were contracted out to seven supplier firms engaged in the production of truck components (see Table 1.2).

Sandouville is a traditional brownfield plant without a long-standing network of suppliers. Thus, Renault developed forms of multi-enterprise organisation by clustering the supplier firms in what they termed an 'industrial hotel'.[4] This can be understood as new *loci* where disciplinary rewards and forms of evaluation govern

Table 1.2   Contracting out in Renault Sandouville

Activities	Employees	Firms
1998–2000		
Head liners	30	Rieter
Seats	323	ISRI
Fuel tanks	40	RotoFrance
Doors	50	Inoplast
Wiring and cabling	30	Lear Corporation
Carpet, door panels, dash boards, consoles	98	Sommer Allibert
Bumpers	50	Plastic Omnium
Total	**621**	

Source: Renault (2001)

the new inter-firm relations. In particular, relationships between Renault and the supplier firms operating within the 'industrial hotel' are regulated by contractual rules. One consequence is that supplier firms' commitment to quality production standards is subordinated to contract rules regulating the transaction between the assembler and the suppliers. Renault's contract rules impose a form of monitoring of the production process through the use of rewards or penalties. Generally speaking, rewards and penalties are determined on the basis of the ability to meet the motor manufacturer's production and quality targets regarding service delivery and/or the production of the product formally established in the contact. Observation at the Renault plant in Sandouville indicated that in the first instance, Renault brought together the supply firms to help them understand the functioning of the new organisation (the 'industrial hotel'). Subsequently, suppliers were encouraged to agree on strategic objectives and even to debate solutions to organisational problems across the network.

This integration impacted very directly on labour relations where there has been a common approach to performance standards and skills profiles notably using appraisal meetings with each supplier in order to evaluate work including discipline and rewards. For instance, a bonus system to boost employee performance motivation was introduced so as to better integrate salaries with notions of supplier service quality. The unions at Renault (especially the Confédération Francaise Démocratique du Travail-CFDT) originally used the information rights of the *comité d'enterprise*, including rights of autonomous expertise, to gain time and elaborate a protection plan for employment benefits as the union's response to industrial reorganisation. However, it is important to note that the low unionisation rate in France (9 per cent) – and even lower at Renault – constrained the unions' scope for extending a negotiated agreement on pay and conditions with management into collective bargaining proper via a formal agreement. By contrast, management sees the reward system as the automatic result of the economic rules regulating contractual inter-firms relationships in the 'industrial hotel'.

Furthermore, one should argue that the reward system, which was introduced into the suppliers to monitor the level of company performance, was also intended to increase the level of employee cohesion in pursuit of Renault's goals (Freyssenet, 1999b). Thus, under the 'industrial hotel' regime, rewards and penalties in turn define the daily conditions of work. Two employees observed:

> We [employees] need to remember that the possibility of being rewarded depends on the ability to deliver good products and to deliver them 'on time' by respecting the contractual conditions requested by Renault (Employee of Renault supplier firm – May, 2001).

> Career depends on the level of performance achieved by the company within the 'industrial hotel' in respect to the goals achieved by the organisation as a result of inter-firm co-operation (Renault employee – May, 2001).

Thus, disciplinary forms of evaluation are introduced to shape and stimulate inter-firm cooperation at the level of the shop floor in the pursuit of Renault's agenda. (Gorgeu and Mathieu, 2005, assessment of the impact of new team working strategies in the French sector, highlight their problematical impact on worker quality of working life). As a supervisor in Renault remarked, the aim is to develop a new system of production that can continuously and autonomously improve the level of the company's performance by linking pay rewards to the level of quality of the service or the product. To sum up, contracting out is identified as an opportunity by Renault to improve production flexibility through economies of specialisation that can reinforce the dependence of its supplier firms. This dependency is driven by monetary calculation and consequently by insecurity amongst suppliers, mindful of the penalties accruing for failure to meet contract obligations. Correspondingly, the effect on employees is one of pressure driven by the obligation to meet Renault's standards.

A brave new world in VW corporation

Volkswagen introduced *ex-novo*, the concept of 'modular consortium' at the greenfield Resende bus and truck plant in Brazil (in the state of Rio de Janeiro), which was inaugurated in June 1996. Modular production at Resende comprises a new pattern of employee organisation within VW's plant where the suppliers (a 'modular consortium' of US, German and Brazilian multinational companies) 'simultaneously manufacture' the truck sequentially and are responsible for the management of their own employees. This means that VW is not involved directly in the manufacturing process because all parts are aggregated together directly on the assembly line by supplier firms. Meanwhile, VW is concerned with strategic functions such as product engineering, marketing and product policies, quality, vehicle design, architecture and sales: 799 out of 1,037 employees are hourly paid and work for eight sub-contracting firms known as *parceiros,* whose size varies according to the complexity and the nature of the product; 200 out of those 799 employees work in maintenance logistics. Very few employees (211 out of 1,037) are salaried shop-floor workers employed directly by VW, 36 of whom are high-level managers (see Table 1.3).

Governance of the modular organisation consists of centralising information and monitoring activities while decentralising responsibility to the *parceiros* for module manufacture. This presupposes tight cooperation between the different parties and in reaching this objective the organisation overcomes the diseconomies of coordination normally associated with arrangements among separate firms (Abreu *et al.,* 2000). The specific pattern of modular organisation at Resende lies in the fact that internal formal relations regulating inter-firm relationships not only shape the modular production flow

Table 1.3   The 'modular consortium' at Resende

Firms	Employees	Product
1996–2000		
Maxion	78	Chassis
Méritor	63	Axles/suspension
Remon	10	Wheels/tyres
Powertrain	56	Engine
VDO	108	Trim
Delga	148	Cabin
Carese	98	Painting
Union Mantein	150	Assembler
Total Tech	40	Maintenance Handling
Partial total	751	
Volkswagen	286	
Total	**1,037**	

Source: Volkswagen (2000)

but also regulate conditions of employment within the *parceiros*. As a VW production manager remarks: *'parceiros* are paid only when the truck is ready to be sold!'.[5] The flow production system makes little space for worker and union involvement and corporate discussion is especially lukewarm about collective bargaining (Ramalho and Santana, 2003). Corporate discussions on wages, benefits and risk-sharing soon became part of the daily management agenda. This is because the 'modular' system implies a division of the risk traditionally wholly assumed by VW and its consortium players. Several interviewees highlighted the implications of risk sharing with respect to employee management. A VDO employee explains: 'those people who are performing well felt they might end up losing since their performance depends on how somebody else performs'. As he sees it, this fuels an incentive to work together to achieve VW's objectives:

> In VW at Resende we share the possibility of receiving a salary. This means that although I do my job well but my colleague in another firm is doing badly at the end of the day VW will not buy that truck! The truck is not ready to be sold yet! Thus, although I did well I will risk as much as my colleague who made a mistake because I am then in danger of not receiving a salary or even worse being sacked. For this reason we help one another, otherwise we would have never been able to make the target! (VDO – paint shop – employee – September, 2000).

VW's modular system pre-empted the inherent conflict in wage disparities between workers of the different companies within the *parceiros* by introducing a common wage and benefits agreement. Intriguingly, this was supported by the dominant union in the plant, *Força Sindical*, a conservative company-union opposed to the socialist *Central Única dos Trabalhadores* (CUT), which dominates the motor industry district, the ABC region, of São Paulo.

In moving to Resende to build up a new pattern of production organisation, the main aim of VW was to avoid the industrial relations 'habits' of the São Paulo region. Resende, an area of high unemployment is where labour relationships are somewhat less conflictual than in the ABC region. This helped to bolster the impression among VW managers that *Força Sindical* would follow the company's lead on all matters. This notion of the 'company-union' became very powerful and was seen as critical in allowing the introduction of the modular consortium's new economic governance rules. This was highlighted right from the start when *Força Sindical* accepted management's opposition to the introduction of the national wage common across the Brazilian automotive industry. However, interestingly, workers were able to accept leverage on each *parceiro* because in meeting the daily production conditions they found a mechanism by which they were able to extract higher wages compared to their colleagues in the ABC region. Nevertheless, one of costs is the extremely limited space for collective representation and notably over the negotiation of employee rights where there is organisational change. This is because employment relations are automatically regulated through the economic rules of 'marketisation' which function to coordinate the various firms at the multi-enterprise level. As a result working conditions and wages and benefits depend on the extent to which the *parceiro* meets VW's requirements. The bargaining power of the social actors is important, except in two telling respects – the 'banking of hours' and the harmonisation of wages. Wage increases within the modular consortium are distributed equally amongst VW and other firms' assembly-line workers to iron out obstacles to production flexibility. Moreover, the introduction of the 'hours bank' was negotiated at plant level with the employee representatives (works councils or *comissão de fábrica*). Generally speaking, the 'hours bank' operates to increase plant-level working time flexibility as it allows the company to reduce or increase working time during an average working week without penalty (either to workers or consortium members).

Further, a crucial aspect to highlight while examining the economic nature of the pillars surrounding the functioning of the modular set-up is that wages are strongly dependent on the profit-sharing system governing the inter-firm relations within the consortium. This is supposed to promote and strengthen the cohesion of workers in the pursuit of capital accumulation. In this context, employees are encouraged to adjust their behaviour in an effort to produce a level of performance compatible with maintaining the overall production process. This increases the pressure on employees 'naturally' because corporate objectives are defined, in monetary terms, as the imperative to sell the truck to the assembler, and therefore produce profit.

Accordingly, the concept of teamwork is redefined by a supervisor in 'Carese' – the paint shop:

> Under the 'modular consortium', 'team' is not the small-medium group of people working in a single company but team means all the *parceiros* working together for selling the truck to VW. This is the new concept of team (Supervisor Carese – September, 2000).

Beneath the thin veneer of sociability and the rhetoric of corporate culture, the concept of market relations governing inter-firm relations under modularity is designed to raise productivity by linking employment arrangements to the profits of the 'modular consortium' as a whole. Generally speaking, the critical pressure driving shop-floor employees to conform to the themes of quality, process improvements and participation in the VW modular system stems from market relations between the various suppliers. These relations are regulated by formal rules by which mutual interdependence between the assembler and the suppliers is ensured. As a VDO supervisor – the trim shop – reported, 'everyone working on the shop floor must look at the indicator shown in the diagram; we must work properly to reach VW targets'. Hence, objective rules rather than the sense of employee loyalty and commitment – or indeed, weak labour union bargaining power – are the critical movers of organisational change at Resende.

Contemporary patterns of firm association in motor manufacturing: 'market' and 'bureaucracy' as the makings of a new production system

As we have argued, during 1990s auto manufacturers worldwide repeatedly sought many of what they took to be principles of Japanese work and production reorganisation. The objective was to increase quality through the creation of a new system of organisation focused on placing human resources and flexible forms of work at the heart of the new management agenda. Accordingly, the shift towards integrated systems of team working, including quality circles, was designed to ensure high productivity and mutual dependency among workers and employers alike. Here, the context is one in which the assembly line is owned by the motor manufacturer, while externalisation of production involves components manufactured by external suppliers.

As the case studies of Fiat, Renault and VW illustrate, since the second half of the 1990s a number of workplaces have been transformed by a complex web of inter-firm relationships characterised by a series of special partnership arrangements impacting directly upon work and employment. The three selected companies see themselves as innovators in the development of forms of contracting out that entail the redefinition of the firm's core activity in the car-manufacturing sector both in Europe and Latin America. These are described as the 'multi-enterprise', or 'modular factory', model and here diversity in the level and complexity of coordinating production activities within each of the manufacturing sites emerges as one of the main findings of the study. To what extent does this diversity impact on employees' perceptions of responsibilities and commitments? Do they tend to see these in terms of the needs of their direct employer or the wider network organisation typical of a multi-enterprise organisation? How far does the development of simultaneously more fragmented and networked organisational forms raise new issues concerning employment regulation and labour control? To what extent are labour unions involved in the regulation of employment under the new transformation in organisation?

First, findings highlight the extent to which automotive manufacturers in these settings seek to reduce responsibility for capital investment through the externalisation of an independently assembled production unit or service. This has been aided by the development of formalised internal agreements among assembler and suppliers at the multi-enterprise settings aimed at devolving even greater responsibility for manufacture to the supplier. Our findings here support Sako and Warburton's (1999) argument that shifting towards multi-enterprise, or 'modular' systems, leads to the generation of a new form of relationship among firms, whereby the boundaries of the industry, including the definition of the business and the risks directly linked to it, are reshaped. Because of the need for on-site coordination of many outsourced operations, the fragmentation of the business can be expected to generate new forms of activity for the organisation which in turn require new ways of managing. The cooperative strength assumed to derive from the modular system includes partnership and contractual arrangements among diverse enterprises, which in turn shape the regulation of labour and employment in the new workplace.

Second, diversity in contracting out places differential emphasis on the elements used to coordinate the production activities within each plant that in turn reflects a varied level of organisational complexity. For sure, all of the plants in the study have been affected by the corporate promotion of synchronous manufacturing on the line as a result of the diverse enterprises operating *in situ*. However, while in Fiat and Renault, coordination of diverse activities was filtered through the vehicle manufacturer holding direct responsibility for parts of the production flow, at VW the assembly line was entirely fragmented with each part under the responsibility of a different enterprise. The difference in the level of organisational complexity has a significant impact on the nature of the monitoring and control of employees within the three car manufacturers and, thereby, underlines diverse approaches to 'marketisation'. While Renault and Fiat are characterised by more conventional forms of 'marketisation' of inter-firm relations (described by Danford, 1997, in another context as 'management by fear') combining elements of post-bureaucratic organisational employee monitoring and control (such as teamwork – again see, Gorgeu and Mathieu, 2005) with economic measures of the level of company performance, at VW by contrast, profit sharing is the rationale pressurising shop-floor employees. Similarities, of course, are important too and notably when we consider the significance of bureaucracy as highlighted at Fiat and Renault where we witnessed the emergence of contractual inter-firm obligations regulated by disciplinary rewards and at VW, where financial arrangements are bureaucratically driven by a profit-sharing rationale. In seeking employee compliance and control, these practices (i.e. discipline rewards, work evaluation and profit-sharing) support the logic of 'marketisation' governing the fragmented organisations. Moreover, as we shall now argue, the control of the labour process takes on greater complexity in multi-enterprise settings requiring changes to the way labour representatives are involved in managing employment concerns.

Regulating employment and workplace representation: a cross-country firm analysis of new patterns of production

While the single employer-employee relationship based around an employment contract is often taken to signify traditional employment relations, the complex and diverse meaning of the employment relationship in the context of multi-enterprise settings poses another set of concerns. As has been emphasised elsewhere, employers bound into inter-firm relationships tend to delegate responsibility for work and production organisation to the suppliers around whom employment relationships are constructed (Thompson and McHugh, 2001). This is important because it is a means of ensuring that the supplier firm has a strong business incentive to ensure manufacturing or service quality. This incentive is exercised through internal formal relations regulating conditions and benefits that are determined largely by the dominant player. In the Brazilian case, for example, it is especially onerous on the supplier who has to accept production schedules and quotas determined by VW. Prior agreement about shared risk may obviously entail losses in production, and profits, in accordance with the whole profit-sharing rationale that each of the parties in the multi-enterprise setting, dominated by VW, has to sign up to.

Whereas the vehicle manufacturer traditionally wholly assumed risk, at VW the component suppliers are involved in a detailed legal and financial relationship with the vehicle manufacturer involving the establishment of medium to long-term production relationships in which the supplier is forced into a dependent relationship. A number of our interviewees highlighted the employee relations implications of the cross-organisational contractual arrangements among firms in VW. Some working for a supplier felt considerable insecurity about the possibility of losing out where somebody else in another enterprise might have been responsible for poor production results. In this context the success of one firm is being increasingly judged by, and dependent upon, the performance of the other firms and this inevitably shapes the nature of the mechanisms through which labour discipline is enacted within the plant. The question then arises as to the role played by employees and their representatives in the regulation of the employment relationship. VW determines the rules of the modular system by dominating wage bargaining. Employee social benefits are subordinated to the emphasis on the inter-firm profit sharing strategy. The unions, in other words, are subordinated to VW's agenda. (See Chapter 6 in this book on VW Resende)

In the less developed cases of modularity at Fiat and Renault, it is disciplinary rewards rather than profit-sharing arrangements that regulate the multi-enterprise settings. More specifically, one might argue that the mechanisms used to achieve labour compliance in the less developed cases of modularity are a mixed variety of labour market tools, providing positive incentives through reward systems and career ladders. Sanctions of course, as we argued, are crucial here. At Fiat and Renault, negative penalties and positive incentives were institutionalised in rules that inspired the behaviour of both managers and employees within each enterprise. To be sure, management control component suppliers and suppliers' employees in much the same way as if they were assembly line production employees working in teams in a (now) conventionally understood lean production plant. This is important in highlighting the way in which monitoring and evaluation are embedded in the fabric of production. A weak production record could jeopardise an extension of the supplier's contract and, of course, employees' benefits, not to mention jobs.

A critical issue here is union and employee involvement in managing the new organisational configurations. The Fiat case presents compelling evidence of union participation in bargaining on the social implications of industrial change. As indicated already, this is contingent upon socio-political and institutional factors, the latter most notably embedded in sector rules governing decentralised workplace relations in Italy. The situation in France is inevitably different and since the mid-1980s, employers, and more especially the state, have supported company-based labour relations. The contrast with Brazil is interesting where the regional structure of the labour market has favoured a highly fragmented national industrial relations system. As a result, labour relations in Brazil are decentralised at plant level and the outcomes of the negotiation process depend on the key role played by employee representatives and works councils. In contrast to France and Brazil, our examination of the Italian automotive sector illustrates union influence over the regulation of labour against a backdrop of restructuring. Nevertheless, despite these variations, research has highlighted a degree of convergence in which contractual arrangements between the different enterprises impact on the regulation of the day-to-day treatment of employees in the plants. In broad terms, it is the economic rules regulating contractual relationships in Fiat – and Renault and VW – as opposed to the negotiation of social issues that have turned out to be the force governing inter-firm and employment relationships in our case studies.

Broadly, in institutional terms we can say that differences notwithstanding, control and involvement from one party or firm in managing the labour process and workers from another firm is crucial in ensuring the required performance level in multi-enterprise settings. This performance level is guaranteed through specific contractual obligations (Renault and Fiat) and financial commitments (VW) which are likely to be imposed for controlling effort levels and quality of work. Thus, in consequence, control of the labour process takes on greater complexity when we move away from direct command and control to a focus on more 'objective' work and employment rules. The monitoring and evaluation of performance, the rewards and discipline of workers through performance assessment and inter-firm financial arrangements are elements defining the economic nature of labour discipline under the 'marketisation'. A significant tendency is for labour representatives to see their role in negotiating employment regulation considerably reduced. Trade union involvement, in other words, is limited to negotiating some basic safeguards (such as working time, skills training, job security and working conditions). In fairness to the unions, it is difficult to see how this marginalisation might be easily transcended. The intention of reorganising production to ensure inter-employer cooperation was primarily based on the need to instil new behavioural patterns specifying performance standards including written definitions of skills. While such systems indicate significant aspects of career development, they are also important in institutionalising values that allow both management and employees specific criteria on which to evaluate worker performance. As part of the new working arrangements, these criteria are generally not negotiated with the unions at company or plant level. Rather, they are experienced by the workforce as part of the new 'natural' set of economic rules governing industrial adjustment. For example, management in Renault has unilaterally developed five formal core standards for performance measurement which, while having an indirect influence on line pacing and direction of work, exert a more obvious impact on monitoring and evaluation, and, consequently, reward and discipline. The core standards are: high product quality, precise delivery time, prompt intervention to correct errors, transparency and, finally, recognition that the supplier company's conduct is indelibly tied to customer perceptions of the vehicle manufacturer. As we have seen, agreed performance standards and skills profiles are used to evaluate work, which includes critical discussion regarding worker reward and discipline.

A number of the middle managers in our three companies considered this organisational link between performance and reward an efficient way to promote the aims of the production network without either direct control of manufacturing operations, or employees' involvement in self-managing activities (such as teamwork). The regulation of the new organisational system therefore requires workers prompt response to the new company-based performance criteria while at the same time isolating the implications of this from the negotiation of employment benefits. This was crucial at Fiat where unions were involved in guaranteeing improved working conditions (including wages) and inter-firm contractual arrangements became the basis for the regulation of employment relations across the Fiat network. This is especially interesting because it contrasts with conventional forms of employee involvement where internalised values of quality, flexibility and value-added activity are considered the basis for gaining competitive organisational advantage. In our case studies, monitoring takes place through the mobilisation of economic indicators measuring company performance while also enabling management to achieve the required level of profitability – the 'market' becomes the new regulatory principle. These economic measures were introduced to shape and stimulate labour control while undermining the involvement of the employee representatives' attempts to negotiate criteria governing the functioning of the new organisational settings. The extent of such involvement is left to the institutional country-based strategies of coordination at industry level characterising the bargaining experience of some southern European countries. Research findings illustrate that in both less and more developed cases of modularity, labour compliance is achieved through the development of economic measures for inter-firm regulation. The differences between the firms, however, are important. While in Fiat and Renault market relations focus primarily on individual contributions to the performance of the company, in VW they are directly embedded in the logic of profit sharing and therefore appear neutral, a product merely of technical necessity naturalised by simultaneous manufacturing (Arbix and Zilbovicius, 1997; Abreu *et al.*, 2000). Generally speaking, multi-enterprise settings in this sector can therefore be seen as allowing an opportunity for the vehicle manufacturer to generate production by reinforcing dependence on either individualised labour market tools (reward systems, career promotion) or financial inter-firm arrangements (profit-sharing) which limit employees and labour representatives' engagement.

Moreover, there is a further aspect that needs to be taken into consideration in order to examine patterns of labour discipline and, thereby, employment regulation in the most advanced form of multi-enterprise environment. In our cases, labour compliance and involvement is achieved to a significant degree through production results measured on the basis of visible performance indicators of quality, output and delivery. Intensive communication across boundaries between middle managers in both vehicle manufacturers and supplier firms supports this activity, which crucially remains outside union control. The degree of effectiveness of this communication impacts upon the ability of the supplier to be competitive while crucially maintaining good relations with the vehicle manufacturer, the main player. Nevertheless, as these research findings suggest, while introducing mechanisms for managing employment relations across employer boundaries may also aspire to instil employees' sense of commitment, the multi-enterprise organisation potentially risks the erosion of informality in the regulation of inter-firm relationships. As Sennett (1998) points out, rather than implying a straightforward rise in centralisation we find increasing complexity in the formality and rigidity of the regulation of employment relations across (and within) diverse subcontractors.

Discussion and conclusion

The ability to sell good products and to link the efficiency of the company's economic performance to individual rewards represents a crucial innovation now embedded in the new manufacturing pattern of production in multi-enterprise organisations in the international motor manufacturing sector. Despite differences in the complexity in the management of inter-firm relations, together with the nature of trade union involvement in managing the social effects of organisational change, the provision of incentives in pursuit of performance standards generates behavioural rules that can reinforce bureaucratic control at work. These contract rules tend to undermine the systems of collective representation as a key factor in the regulation of employment relationships in our context. Thus, intriguingly, the use of bureaucratic control emerges as the main element of labour control in this type of workplace in so far as it is filtered through a complex web of inter-firm relationships driven by market rationale. The logic of the market has the effect of appearing to naturalise competition. The latter is then seen as regulator of economic and social relationships within (and among) firms.

Performance evaluation and reward and discipline at Fiat, VW and Renault were associated with bureaucratic control in Edwards' sense (1979). This is important since it highlights the extent to which the conception of bureaucracy, beyond the internal structures of a corporation, now includes activities dispersed to those firms employed to provide services and production to another firm. This account stands in contrast to arguments that see the emergence through networks of a new anti-bureaucratic production system that empowers workers. The experience of workers in the four factories is quite different from this. Here it seems that a modular production system based on a network of diverse subcontractors accelerated rather than reduced the tendency towards centralisation and rigid formal rules.

Despite divergence in the way new designs of the production, process were implemented under multi-enterprise settings. What appears to be common here is that for most of the managers in our research, incentives and career advancement were used to inculcate behavioural patterns under the auspices of bureaucratic control. Here, values, beliefs and standards of attainment and assessment for each distinctive organisation were utilised to enforce employee conformity, unit and departmental performance targets. This was seen to be crucial to the maintenance of employment at the subcontractor. The situation at multi-enterprise workplaces in other words, is one in which the practical process of bureaucratic control emerges – 'objective' performance information is combined with 'objective' bureaucratic standards to evaluate and reward work. Compulsion to work is generally mobilised where there is an increased role for calculative incentives that reward individual performance on the basis of quality and delivery. In this scenario, employees are categorised and socially regulated so as to advance their usefulness within the organisation (Burawoy, 1979; Littler, 1982). Evidence shows that much of the cooperation in the multi-enterprise context arises, seemingly paradoxically, from companies' competing efforts to achieve 'objective' measures that can be used to manage employment relations across firms. Moreover, despite internal monitoring of output in each company, many employees were concerned to maximise bonuses and to cooperate in enabling their company to respond positively to the vehicle manufacturer's production requests. Here, the relationship between control and efficient operations is revealed through employees' concerns that any negative feedback would lead to heavy sanctions as a result of the reward-punishment system governing their organisation. Moreover, as managers at VW report, evaluation is also integrated through the use of economic devices such as profit sharing which is part of the incentive system designed by management to achieve high performance and induce cooperation across suppliers. Thus, without the incentive system, suppliers would otherwise be forever castigating one another for slowing or otherwise undermining the overall production process. Hence, performance targets aim to provide a means of working 'smarter' under the recent changes in the industry. This is significant also because it serves to highlight the seemingly ironic way in which the shift from traditional rule-governed behaviour can lead to a renewal of bureaucratic processes.

Acknowledgements

The authors thank the Italian Ministry for Research (MUIR) which funded the research, Fiat-auto, Renault and Volkswagen and the trade unions federations CGIL in Italy, CGT in France and CUT in Brazil for collaborating in arranging interviews.

Notes

1   The research was conducted prior to the recent decision by Fiat in 2002 to transfer production from Rivalta to Mirafiori. Fiat's closure of Rivalta followed the short-term alliance with GM, now ended.
2   Each UTE is responsible for quality control, variance absorption, self-control and continuous improvement of a single segment of the production process.
3   Interview TNT employee – June, 2000.
4   'Industrial Hotel' is the expression used at Renault in order to indicate the cluster of firms (vehicle manufacturer and suppliers) operating on the same shop floor.
5   Interview with a VW Production Manager – August, 2000.

References

Abreu, A., Beynon, H. and Ramalho, R. (2000) 'The Dream Factory': VW's Modular Production System in Resende, Brazil', *Work, Employment and Society*, 14: 265–82.

Appelbaum, E., Bailey, T., Berg, T. and Kalleberg, A.L. (2000) *Manufacturing Advantage*, Ithaca: Cornell University Press.

Arbix, G. and Zilbovicius, M. (1997) 'Consórcio Modular da VW: um Novo Modelo de Produç*o?' in Arbix, G. Zilbovicius, M. *et al.*, *De JK a FHC, a Reigeneraç*o do Carros*, São Paulo: Scritta.

Barker (1999) 'Tightening the Iron Cage: Concertive Control in Self-managing Teams', *Administrative Science Quarterly*, 38: 408–37.

Bonazzi, G. and Antonelli, C. (2003) 'To Make or to Sell? The Case of In-House Outsourcing at Fiat-Auto', *Organisation Studies*, 24(4): 575–94.

Burawoy, M. (1979) *Manufacturing Consent*. Chicago: University of Chicago.

Danford, D. (1997) 'The "New Industrial Relations" and Class Struggle in the 1990s', *Capital and Class*, 61: 107–41.

Du Gay, P. and Salaman, G. (1992) 'The Culture of the Customer', *Journal of Management Studies*, 29: 615–33.

Edwards, R. (1979) *Contested Terrain: the Transformation of the Workplace in the Twentieth Century*. London: Heinemann Educational.

Freyssenet, M. (1999a) 'Transformations in Teamwork at Renault' in Durand, J.P., Stewart, P. and Castillo, J., *Teamwork in the Automobile Industry*. London: MacMillan.

Freyssenet, M. (1999b) 'Emergence, Centrality and the End of Work', *Current Sociology*, 47.

Gorgeu, A. and Mathieu, R. (2005) 'Teamwork in Factories within the French Automobile Industry', *New Technology, Work and Employment*, 20: 2, 88–101.

Kunda, G. (1992) *L'ingegneria della Cultura. Controllo, Appartenenza e Impegno in un'Impresa ad Alta Tecnologia*. Milan: Ed. Comunità.

Lash, S. and Urry, J. (1987) The End of Organised Capitalism. Oxford: Polity Press.

Littler, C.R. (1982) *The Development of Labour Process in Capitalist Societies*. London: Heinemann.

Ouchi, W.G. (1981) *Theory Z: How American Business Can Meet the Japanese Challenge*. New York: Addison-Wesley.

Parker, M. (1999) 'Capitalism, Subjectivity and Ethics: Debating Labour Process Analysis', *Organisation Studies*, 20: 25–45.

Piore, M. and Sabel, J. (1984) *The Second Industrial Divide: Possibilities for Prosperities*. New York: Basic Books.

Pulignano, V. (2005) 'Union responses to 'multi-enterprise' factories in the Italian motor industry', *Industrial Relations Journal*, 36(2): 157–73.

Ramalho, J.R. and Santana, M.A. (2003) 'Volkswagen's Modular System, Regional Development and Workers' Organization in Resende, Brazil' in Charron E. and Stewart P. (ed.) Work and Employment Relations in the Automobile Industry. London: Palgrave Macmillan.

Ray, C. (1986) 'Corporate Culture: The Last Frontier of Control', Journal of Management Studies, 23: 287–97.

Sako, M. and Warburton, M. (1999) Modularisation and Outsourcing Project Interim of European Research Team, IMVP Annual Forum, MIT, Boston, 6–7 October.

Sennett, R. (1998) The Corrosion of Character. New York: W.W. Norton.

Thompson, P. (1983) The Nature of Work. An Introduction to Debates on Labour Process. London: MacMillan.

Thompson, P. and Findlay, P. (1999) 'Changing the People: Social Engineering in the Contemporary Workplace' in Ray, L. and Sayer, A. Culture and Economy after Cultural Turn. London: Sage Publications.

Thompson and McHugh (2001) Work Organisation. London: Palgrave Macmillan.

Townley, B. (1993) 'Foucault, Power/Knowledge and its Relevance for Human Resource Management', Academy of Management Review, 18: 159–545.

Vallas, S. (1999) 'Rethinking Post-Fordism, The Meaning of Workplace Flexibility', Sociological Theory, March: 68–101.

Van Mannen, J. and Kunda, G. (1989) 'Real Feelings: Emotional Expression and Organisational Culture' in Cunnings, L. and Staw, B. (eds) Research in Organisational Behavior, vol. 2. Greenwich Conn.: JAI Press.

Willmott, H. (1993) 'Strength is Ignorance; Slavery is Freedom: Managing Culture in Modern Organisation', Journal of Management Studies, 30: 515–52.

Wilkinson, A. and Willmott, H. (1995) Making Quality Critical: New Perspectives on Organisational Change. London: Routledge.

2

Lean Production and Quality of Working Life on the Shop Floor: The Experience of British and Italian Car Workers

Andy Danford, Mike Richardson, Valeria Pulignano and Paul Stewart

Introduction

In this chapter, we present survey data of different dimensions of employee experience of life on the lean production line in three European car plants. Our core research question is to interrogate the central employee-centred claim of the original IMVP researchers. That is, lean manufacturing offers something better for workers (compared to the rigours of Fordist/Taylorist production systems) in that the 'working smarter' mantra encapsulates a process that provides the space and management techniques to establish more participative (and less stressful) work environments:

> While the mass-production plant is often filled with mind-numbing stress, as workers struggle to assemble unmanufac-turable products and have no way to improve their working environment, lean production offers a creative tension in which workers have many ways to address challenges. This creative tension involved in solving complex problems is precisely what has separated manual factory work from professional "think" work in the age of mass production' (Womack *et al.*, 1990: 101).

Our research data explore a number of inter-linked themes concerning the impact of shifts in the labour process and employment relations under lean production regimes. Specifically, we question a number of assumptions governing the effects of lean manufacturing techniques on employee well-being at the workplace level. For instance, the utility of new cooperative industrial relations systems, the extent of employee autonomy – and management surveillance – on the assembly line, and the condition of productive labour measured by such material factors as changes in workload levels, work ergonomics, the intensity and speed of work and reported levels of stress.

Our analysis exposes a substantial gap between the rhetoric of lean production and workers' lived experiences on the line. For example: limited worker consultation and participation; a lack of employee autonomy and discretion; and a degradation of employment conditions manifest in patterns of labour intensification through conventional means (speeding up the line and cutting staffing levels) and associated problems of managerial surveillance and worker stress. We conclude that when viewed in conjunction with the many critical studies that follow the labour process tradition, our data highlight the shortcomings of the lean production paradigm, underpinned as it is by a 'technologist' conception of history and a position that is consequently neutral in terms of class relations and shop-floor conflict.

The politics of lean production: the cases of BMW-Cowley, GM-Vauxhall and Fiat-Melfi

A downturn in the global economy in the early 1990s exacerbated the already difficult operating environment in the automobile market. Thus, as competitive pressures intensified automobile manufacturers were compelled to react, which many did by re-evaluating and reforming their organisational strategies and industrial relations policies. This was the case at BMW-Cowley and GM-Vauxhall in England and Fiat-Melfi in Italy.

BMW-Cowley

BMW-Cowley was born out of the turbulent and troubled history of the Rover Group. In 1975, Rover was part of the British Leyland Motor Corporation (BLMC) that was threatened with bankruptcy. Concerned about the negative impact that such an event would have on the British economy, the Labour government stepped in and took control of the company. There followed a period of relent-less restructuring, under the direction of the company chairman, Michael Edwardes, which resulted in a reduction of the workforce from 186,000 in 1978 to 46,000 in 1988. The car division of BLMC became known as the Rover Group. In 1988 the company was privat-ised, when, somewhat surprisingly, British Aerospace took control. It carried out a series of further cuts and began systemising lean pro-duction techniques, first introduced in the period of BLMC's alli-ance with Honda earlier in the 1980s. This, in parallel with exacting union support, paved the way for the 'Rover Tomorrow' agreement in 1992. In contrast to the 1989 agreement at Vauxhall, despite much opposition on the shop floor, unions accepted and agreed to promote increased flexibility and a series of new working practices, taking the view that management would impose these changes if the union failed to agree. Consequently, the unions secured the agreement of their respective memberships, albeit by a tiny major-ity, to accept the 'deal' by raising the company's threat of union de-recognition and emphasizing how the agreement included clauses on no lay-offs and no enforced redundancies. Following, this ground-breaking agreement Rover's market share fell significantly and in 1994 British Aerospace readily sold its share of the business to BMW.

Upon taking the company over, BMW took full advantage of the 'Rover Tomorrow' agreement by embarking on a process of conces-sion bargaining. Cultural differences between the UK and German systems of industrial relations emerged (Eckardt and Klemm, 2003; Tuckman and Whittall, 2006). These differences reached a climax in 1997 when BMW made further investment in Rover's Longbridge plant dependent on the acceptance of partnership principles drawn from Germany's co-determination model, as well as agreeing to significant changes in work practices (Tuckman and Whittall, 2006). Among the most unwelcome demands were the mobility of labour between production plants; a working-time account (annualised hours); and changes to work routines and shift patterns. In 1998, agreements to this end were reached with the unions but nego-tiations were carried out in secret for reasons of confidentiality, a feature of workplace partnership. Initially, Rover shop stewards found this commitment to confidentiality hard to accept and alien to the way they had previously conducted industrial relations.

However, they felt they had little alternative. If investment was not forthcoming they felt that the 1992 guarantee of no enforced redundancies, known as 'jobs for life', was likely to be withdrawn. Critically, discussions over changes in work practices were conducted outside the ambit of wage reviews and therefore not dependent on the company offering monetary compensation, a key factor of the lean production model, and a direct result of 'working in partnership'. In this new environment the evidence suggests that the unions felt they had little option other than to accept the changes rather than mobilise opposition.

In the event, the promise of job security in return for union co-operation proved to be illusory. Job losses numbering 2,500 eventually followed the 1998 agreement and two years later, on 16 March 2000, the decision was made to hive off the Longbridge plant to four businessmen, known as the Phoenix Four, for the princely sum of £10. Production of the new Mini was transferred from the Longbridge plant in Birmingham to the Cowley plant in Oxford (its engine was built in Brazil) enabling BMW to keep the Mini brand within the BMW group. A new flexible working system was introduced at Cowley, in 2001, in order to meet customer demand in the built-to-order market. Rover, now the last British-owned volume car maker, went into administration in April 2005, with the loss of over 5,000 jobs.

GM-Vauxhall

In the late 1980s, GM-Vauxhall embarked on a staged introduction of lean production. Part of GM's long-term strategy was to integrate its UK plants with GM Europe in an effort to bring production costs and quality in line with its best-performing plants (Arrowsmith, 2002). To achieve this, workers from different plants were compelled to compete with each other for work and new investment. Those securing the most competitive union agreements apropos pay and flexibility were better placed to retain existing work or acquire new work. This 'survival of the fittest' strategy was particularly effective in periods of over capacity, a feature of the automobile industry in the last twenty years or more. This strategy facilitated the drive to lean production. The 1989 agreement was the first step in this process. For GM-Vauxhall management this was a new strategy and, therefore, the gradual evolution of lean was considered as the best way forward. The company concluded that given the presence of strong trade union traditions and organisation it was shrewd to get the unions onside by taking such an approach. By 1989, compared with the early 1970s, the power relations pendulum between management and trade unions both in the UK and within the company had swung another degree in favour of the former. Thus, the company seized the opportunity to secure the introduction of key elements of lean production, especially continuous improvement and the formation of joint problem solving committees in their negotiations with the trade unions. However, the TGWU, in particular, was not unprepared, despite its weakened position *vis-à-vis* management. It entered into negotiations in 1989 on the basis of 'engaging with change rather than embracing change'; although this term was not coined to characterise union strategy until the Luton *'Working Together to Win'* agreement was struck in 1992. In exchange for a more flexible approach to industrial relations from the unions, and their undertaking to support continuous improvement, the company gave assurances on job security. In an effort to keep these agreements in check, the TGWU, drawing on its strong traditions of rank-and-file involvement, set about raising membership awareness of the dangers of being beguiled by management rhetoric to develop GM's policy of 'Jointism' by way of lean techniques such as kaizen and team briefings (Stewart, 1997).

By 1995, however, it was clear to the GM-Vauxhall workforce that lean production methods were operating to their detriment, particularly in regard to increases in work intensification. 'The irony for the unions was that this pressure for change had grown as a direct consequence both of their own proactive strategy of direct engagement with the politics and ideology of lean production and workers own experiences of the reality of so-called 'smarter work' (Stewart, 1997). The extent of worker discontent at GM-Vauxhall was revealed in 1995 when the majority of assembly workers indicated in a ballot that they were prepared to take strike action in pursuance of a shorter working week and improvements in pay and conditions. They demanded some return on the productivity improvements they had delivered since the introduction of lean productions techniques. That they achieved an hour's reduction in the working week was a mark of the strength of organised labour at GM-Vauxhall but the unions, in striking a three year deal, settled for less than that advocated by the shop-floor. This gave room for the company to pursue the implementation of the central objectives of lean without too much fear of major industrial disruption from its workforce. The step by step approach towards implementing lean was beginning to bring dividends for management.

Before the end of the 1995 agreement, in 1997, negotiations had commenced on the composition of a new agreement. By this time the threat of closure over the UK Luton plant loomed large. As one Ellesmere Port worker we interviewed recalled: 'We were told during wage negotiations that the only way to save the plant [Luton] was to accept a pay deal that to say the least was not up to scratch'. The UK unions were drawn fully into European wide concession bargaining, the conclusion of a process that had begun nearly a decade earlier. Key union concessions in a three year pay and productivity package included working time flexibility (the beginning of annualised hours); a three shift system; the use of temporary workers; reduced starting pay for new production workers (82.5 per cent of the full rate); and the adoption of the latest lean manufacturing techniques (Arrowsmith, 2002). In return the company gave assurances that there would be no plant closures in the UK and no compulsory redundancies.

Fiat-Melfi

In the early 1990s, Fiat embarked on a major organisational transformation entailing a shift from Fordist mass production which was predominant during the period 1955 to 1980, to an automation strategy (Highly Automated Factory) in the 1980s designed to reduce labour costs and union influence, to a new paradigm grounded on the principles of the lean production model (Camuffo and Volpato, 1998). The new greenfield site at Melfi opened in 1993 and was subject to this new paradigm.

A particularly acrimonious industrial dispute in 1980 culminated in a weakening of union strength at Fiat. After 1985, the unions regained some of their lost influence (as the demand for cars increased) but this was based on concession bargaining, a process that resulted in the approval of increased worker flexibility. The company took advantage of this development during the economic downturn in the early 1990s to forge new partnership relations with the major unions. The logic of this strategy was that it gave legitimacy to the planned changes in work organisation in new production plants to be opened in southern Italy. The success of this new venture was dependent on union support (Camuffo and Volpato, 1998). The top-down structure of workplace unionism in Italy facilitated the framing of a partnership-based agreement that traded the creation of new jobs in southern Italy for union acceptance of 'becoming the "guardian and guarantors" of the company's productivity' (Patriotta and Lanzara, 2006: 993). Workplace representation was channelled through RSU (rappresentanza sindacale unitaria).

In Italy, workers have a legal right to establish workers' representatives (RSU), two thirds of which are elected by workers and one third nominated by the relevant union organisations. Hence, unions are assured of representation even in workplaces with low union densities. At the new Melfi plant, therefore, workplace representation was channelled through internal and external delegates in what could be called an arranged marriage between the union bureaucracy and rank-and-file delegates. RSU representatives sat on joint consultative committees which were set up by the company to promote positive social dialogue (Pulignano, 2002a).

This has been the representational arrangement since production began at Melfi. Effectively unions agreed not to interfere with managerial prerogatives. Consequently, Fiat management was able to introduce its vision of lean manufacturing at Melfi without union hindrance and hire a young workforce from the rural locality. Each individual was vetted to ensure their social traits matched Fiat's requirements – loyal, cooperative, less than 32 years of age, and able to work under pressure – in short 'appropriate' individuals (Camuffo and Volpato, 1998: 328).

Before car production commenced at the Melfi plant in 1993, 1,000 novice, but well-educated, workers were recruited and put through a programme of intense training. Once trained in the 'Fiat method' these workers contributed to the construction of the Melfi plant and practised, and assimilated, 'the correct way' for assembling cars, which was to become the template for future production. The initial aim was to secure a committed, loyal and highly skilled team able to pass on company values and knowledge of car assembly to a new workforce. The key objective was to formalise and codify work methods for the new workforce to follow. Once the factory was fully operational a 'technology-based model' with rules and regulation of

production materialised (Lanzara and Patriotta, 2007). This Tayloristic approach formed the basis for the lean production model and
just-in-time working with component suppliers operating on site
under a system of congruent working conditions and industrial relations (Pulignano, 2002b). Fundamental to this new model, labelled
the Integrated Factory (IF), were manufacturing cells known as
Elementary Technical Units (UTEs) the level at which teamworking
functioned. The deployment of workers in these UTE cells was aimed
partially at achieving a mix of skilled and unskilled labour responsible
for a segment of assembly operations. Each UTE would integrate
production technologists with assembly workers, running continuous
improvements activities and acting as internal customers to the pre-
ceding UTE on the production line (Camuffo and Volpato, 1998;
Lanzara and Patriotta, 2007). Equally, the goal was to codify workers'
tacit knowledge into a set of tightly supervised working practices in
order to reduce idle time and improve productivity and product
quality (Pulignano, 2002b). Each UTE is responsible for a specific
production process and comprises between 20–25 members in the
smallest unit to 75–80 in the largest. A key objective of UTEs was to
direct task decision-making to the lowest level of the organisation.
Camuffo and Volpato (1998: 330) argue, however, that at best a hybrid
form of IF applied as often 'the traditional hierarchical practice' prevailed whilst union-management committees declined. Moreover,
Pulignano (2002a: 86) in her study found that despite labour compliance (as a consequence of JIT), there was still 'a great deal of
mistrust and defensiveness on the shop-floor.'

The common denominator in these three automotive companies
is the tightening of the screw of compliance on trade unions and
their members. This was more apparent at Fiat where a formal
employer-dominant partnership agreement had been in place since
the Melfi plant opened in 1993. At BMW a weaker partnership
developed first as a result of crisis (that is, company survival) and
then, under the new BMW ownership, union acceptance of certain
stakeholder features of co-determination practised by the parent
company. At GM-Vauxhall, despite the claim by Arrowsmith (2002)
that management and trade unions were talking in partnership
terms, evidence from the workplace reveals that a more adversarial
form of collective bargaining prevailed at the plant level. However,
even in this more oppositionalist plant the balance of power mostly

favoured the employer enabling management to gradually push through radical changes.

The analysis presented in this chapter is based upon research data collected at three plants: Cowley, UK (BMW-Cowley), Ellesmere Port, UK (GM-Vauxhall) and Melfi, Italy (Fiat). The data were collected from the UK plants in 2001 and from Melfi in 2003. Survey questionnaires were distributed to sample populations of 200 direct and indirect production workers at each plant. These were based in a variety of production functions but mostly in the trim, paint and body shop sections. Response rates were: BMW-Cowley (Rover), 73 responses (37 per cent); GM-Vauxhall, 100 responses (50 per cent) and Fiat, 71 responses (36 per cent).

Our analytical framework comprised a number of research questions that questioned the lean rhetoric of decentralisation and power from below:

1. In the context of the supposed shift from control to commitment in lean management philosophy, and the associated processes of cooperation and partnership in workplace relations, how do workers in these lean regimes rate their managers' performance in supporting company consultation and employee welfare?
2. In the context of different sets of management-union relationships at the three plants, how do workers rate their unions' performance in communication and engagement with management agendas?
3. In the context of the supposed shift from Tayloristic control to worker discretion, does the lived experience of manual work on the lean production line accord with management's 'working smarter' rhetoric and associated assumptions about 'worker empowerment'? Specifically, how do workers evaluate their exposure to the basic conditions on the line and shifting labour standards governing such questions as workload and work speed?
4. Finally, to what extent are associated relational issues such as the real extent of employee autonomy, workplace stress and managerial bullying potential problems for these car workers?

Worker attributes

Table 2.1 provides a summary of the attributes of the British and Italian workers who participated in the survey. A number of these

Table 2.1   **Attributes of survey respondents**

Worker attributes	BMW	GM	FIAT
Average age (yrs)	44	41	32
Average experience (yrs)	20	17	7
Average weekly hours	39	38	41
Men (%)	93	94	89
Women (%)	7	6	11
Direct workers (%)	67	73	79
Indirect workers (%)	33	27	21
Relations in plant (%)	45	51	33
Active in union (%)	64	78	51

reflect the contrasting labour force characteristics of brownfield and greenfield manufacturing plants. For example, both British plants had an ageing workforce. The combined average age was 42 years (only 10 per cent of respondents were aged under 30) whilst average length of employment at the plants was 18 years. At the relatively new Fiat plant, the age and service profile was predictably different: average age was just over 30 whilst average service was almost two thirds less than the British cases. The gender profile of the three work-forces reflected deeply entrenched gender segmentation patterns in automotive manufacture (the number of women respondents in the survey amounted to little more than one in 20). Recruitment practices corresponded to the traditions associated with paternalistic manage-ment and close ties between the plants and their local communities in that a good number of workers had family members and other rela-tives who also worked in the plant. Over three quarters of respondents were categorised as direct workers, mainly assembly and body shop workers, whilst the remainder were indirect workers (forklift drivers and other shop-floor labourers). Finally, relatively high proportions of workers classed themselves as active union members – active in the sense of regularly attending union meetings, discussing issues with shop stewards, reading union newsletters, and so on. The proportion was significantly higher in the British plants where the locales and respective histories and collective memories of strong union organ-isation were more likely to generate a resilient trade union conscious-ness on the shop floor.

As far as work organisation and skill were concerned, nearly 60 per cent of workers reported that they were deployed in some form of production team. And despite the optimistic claims of those lean management gurus who proclaim a new, post-Taylorist manufacturing environment, few workers held any delusions over the skill content of their work. Over 70 per cent of workers felt that it would take less than a month to train someone to do their job and over 40 per cent felt it would just take a few days or less. At the GM plant, as many as 25 per cent of workers felt that it would take just a few hours. Also, the use of rotating shifts (a week of days followed by a week of nights) was standard practice at the GM and Fiat plants. In our sample, 75 per cent of workers at GM and 83 per cent at Fiat worked such patterns (at BMW the figure was much lower at 15 per cent). This is a high proportion given that such shift patterns are likely to be a causal risk factor in the stress-coronary heart disease mechanism (Mayhew, 2003).

Workplace partnership and management and union performance

The questionnaire survey incorporated a number of questions that explored employee assessment of the performance of their managers and unions in the regulation of the employment relationship. In the context of the three sets of management-union relationships at the plant level that we described above (what might be termed 'strong' institutional partnership at Fiat, 'weak' partnership at BMW and something more akin to adversarial relations at GM), the analysis was able to focus on potential contrasts between workers subject to these different relationships, as well as general trends. Respondents were asked two sets of management questions. The first governed management involvement in consulting employees about new work practices and work reorganisation and to what extent employees felt consulted over company policy. The second set were related to the issue of 'respect' in asking employees whether they felt management policies at their workplace were reasonable and fair and whether management was interested in their welfare. These are central themes in the supposed shift from control to commitment in new management philosophy (Gallie *et al.*, 2001; Hodson, 2001). They also take on a particular resonance in the light of the supposed importance of these issues for the development of

Table 2.2 Workers' assessment of consultation and respect at work (row percentages)

| | How involved has management been in telling you about new practices & work reorganisation? | | | |
	Very involved	Involved	Not very involved	Not involved at all
All	3	32	41	24
BMW	3	47	33	17
GM	5	35	41	19
Fiat	1	12	48	39

| | To what extent do you feel consulted over company policy? | | | | |
	Great deal	A lot	Some	A little	None
All	2	3	18	22	55
BMW	1	3	29	24	43
GM	4	6	21	24	45
Fiat	0	0	4	16	80

| | Are management policies reasonable and fair at this workplace? | | | | |
	Very fair	Fair	Neither	Unfair	Very unfair
All	1	23	26	33	17
BMW	1	38	23	31	7
GM	1	27	37	29	6
Fiat	0	3	14	40	43

| | How interested is management in your welfare? | | | | |
	Very interested	Interested	Not sure	Not very interested	Not interested at all
All	2	17	26	33	22
BMW	3	27	23	27	20
GM	2	18	31	26	23
Fiat	1	7	22	49	21

partnership in contemporary workplace relations (Coupar and Stevens, 1998; Heery, 2002).

The results are shown in Table 2.2. For the two British plants these suggest patterns of management activity in employee consultation but predominant worker dissatisfaction with the results. Overall, just under a half of BMW and GM respondents felt that management had been involved in consulting them about work organisational change. The proportion was higher in BMW's 'weak partnership' setting. However, when asked whether they felt consulted over company policy a more negative pattern emerged. Over two thirds of BMW and GM respondents responded either 'a little' or 'none' and there was no obvious difference between the two plants. These negative patterns were starker still in the Fiat plant governed by 'strong partnership'. Only 13 per cent of these Italian workers felt that their managers were involved in consultation whilst a full 80 per cent indicated that they were never consulted over company policy.

A similar UK-Italian contrast emerged in worker responses to the 'respect' questions. In the British plants, sizeable minorities of workers felt that their management's policies were reasonable and fair although BMW workers were more likely than their non-partnership GM counterparts to indicate positively. On the other hand, in both plants workers held more cynical attitudes concerning management's interest in their welfare: nearly 50 per cent of respondents felt that their managers were not interested. In the greenfield Fiat plant, the pattern of worker responses was again far more negative: 83 per cent felt that their management's policies were unfair whilst 70 per cent felt that management was not interested in their welfare.

We explored further facets of these employee responses by creating a 'management performance' summative scale based on the last three questions in Table 2.2. Responses were coded from four to zero with a great deal/very fair/very interested coded as four. This group of questions had an internal consistency reliability (Cronbach's Alpha) of 0.732. Table 2.3 presents the mean scores for the scale.

The results confirm that workers in the three plants tended to have a poor assessment of their managers' performance governing the respect agenda. Moreover, whilst differences between management performance in the 'weak partnership' BMW plant and more conventional GM plant were minimal (although we might have expected more positive management performance scores at BMW) there were significant differences between these plants and the 'strong partnership' Fiat plant. There were also significant differences between age groups with younger workers more likely to rate management performance lower.

Table 2.3   Management performance scale

	Management Performance Mean Score (0–12)
BMW	4.57
GM	4.33
Fiat	2.20
Aged 18–30 yrs	2.19
Aged 31–40 yrs	3.40
Aged 41–50 yrs	4.46
Aged 51–65 yrs	4.81
Direct workers	3.44
Indirect workers	4.42
Active union members	3.73
Non-active union members	3.65

The same applies to direct workers deployed on the production lines compared to indirect workers.

The survey also explored worker assessments of trade union performance at the three plants. In this case, three related questions were adopted. Mirroring the 'management involvement' question, respondents were asked how involved their unions had been in communicating about work organisational change. They were also asked how involved their unions had been in getting management to modify work practices and in trying to improve health and safety conditions. Taken together, the questions provided a rudimentary index of union engagement with the 'micro-politics' of lean production. As Table 2.4 shows, overall, 44 per cent of workers felt that their union had been involved in communicating about work organisational change compared to 35 per cent who felt that management had been involved. In addition, relatively large proportions of workers rated union involvement highly with regard to modifying work practices and improving health and safety. However, these overall results masked some stark inter-plant differences. Workers in the non-partnership GM plant were far more likely to indicate that their unions had been very involved on all three counts compared to BMW and Fiat. Moreover, in the Fiat plant where partnership was firmly institutionalised in extensive

Table 2.4   Workers' assessment of union performance at work (row percentages)

	How involved has the union been in telling you about new practices & work reorganisation?			
	Very involved	Involved	Not very involved	Not involved at all
All	13	31	32	24
BMW	7	37	35	21
GM	26	36	27	11
Fiat	2	16	34	48

	How involved has the union been in getting management to modify work practices?			
	Very involved	Involved	Not very involved	Not involved at all
All	24	44	23	9
BMW	20	53	20	7
GM	38	47	11	4
Fiat	7	31	44	17

	How involved has the union been in trying to improve health and safety conditions?			
	Very involved	Involved	Not very involved	Not involved at all
All	31	38	22	9
BMW	21	58	13	8
GM	57	31	9	3
Fiat	3	27	51	19

management-union committee structures the unions were much more likely to receive a negative assessment.

A union performance' scale was created based on the three questions. Responses to each were coded from 3 (very involved) to zero (not involved at all). This group of questions had an internal consistency reliability (Cronbach's Alpha) of 0.8600. Mean scores are presented in Table 2.5. The results confirmed large and statistically significant differences between workers' assessment of union performance in the three plants. Whilst the scale of UK-Italian differences might be partly attributable to different worker expectations of the

Table 2.5   Union performance scale

	Union Performance Mean Score (0–9)
BMW	5.09
GM	6.35
Fiat	3.07
Aged 18–30 yrs	3.83
Aged 31–40 yrs	4.68
Aged 41–50 yrs	5.95
Aged 51–65 yrs	6.39
Direct workers	5.01
Indirect workers	5.25
Active union members	5.69
Non-active union members	3.71

traditional role of workplace unions the differences between GM and the two partnership plants provide further evidence that unions which reject partnership and engage more critically with new management initiatives are more likely to garner rank and file support (see for example Danford *et al.*, 2005 and 2007; Kelly 2004).

Table 2.5 also highlights a number of differences between sub-groups of employees. In line with their ratings of management performance, younger workers tended to view the extent of union involvement less positively than older workers. This result was partly distorted by the 'Italian effect' (there were more younger workers in the Fiat sub-set), nevertheless, perhaps it reflects also a pattern of youth-related alienation from the rigour and monotony of life on the lean production assembly line. There was also a significant difference between active and non-active union members. This difference is interesting in that active members were more likely to be based in the non-partnership GM plant (78 per cent) compared to BMW (65 per cent) and Fiat (51 per cent). In the latter cases, one reading of these results is that partnership relations may be acting to gradually undermine (or in the case of Fiat, constrain the emergence of) forms of independent workplace unionism based on grassroots member participation.

Working conditions and workload

One of the core tenets of lean doctrine is that compared to conventional 'Fordist' work organisation, lean manufacturing systems can generate greater labour productivity via a more sophisticated management of the indeterminacy of labour. The distinctive technological and relational components of lean production, such as just-in-time and teamworking, are assumed to generate higher trust between employees and managers along with the prospects for greater worker autonomy and empowerment on the shop floor. Towards the end of the last century many employers attempted to subvert worker resistance to the imperatives of lean production by the use of 'factory survival' productivity campaigns. These often adopted the trite maxim 'working smarter rather than harder' and were supported by IMVP researchers (Womack *et al.*, 1990; see also MacDuffie, 1995, 1999). There was also a great deal of interest in the work of the 'Japanisation school', such as Kenney and Florida (1993), who argued that the competitive edge of Japanese forms of lean production lay in 'innovation-mediated production'. Essentially, this was a new relational framework that attempted to harness the job knowledge of design and production engineers and shop-floor workers.

In the next two sections we provide an alternative picture that runs counter to this 'empowerment' rhetoric. This is based on an analysis of car workers' direct experiences of the lean production line. We consider in turn, basic conditions on the line, workload and work speed before moving on to different dimensions of quality of working life, such as employee autonomy, workplace stress and bullying.

The survey explored the theme of work intensity by adopting questions on staffing levels, workload and the pace of production. Respondents were asked whether they felt there was sufficient people in their work area to cover the work assigned to them, whether there was an adequate number of relief staff to enable them to leave the job to attend to personal matters, such as, going to the toilet, and a further three questions related to workload levels, time available to complete work tasks and the pace of work. The results are presented in Table 2.6.

The first pattern to emerge is that although substantial numbers of workers felt that staffing levels were about right (though very few

Table 2.6   Workers' assessment of workload (row percentages)

	Enough people in your work area to cover the work assigned?		
	Too many or far too many	About right	Too few or far too few
All	7	41	52
BMW	3	37	60
GM	5	47	48
Fiat	13	36	51
	Adequate relief staff in your area?		
	Too many or far too many	About right	Too few or far too few
All	3	37	60
BMW	3	42	55
GM	0	44	56
Fiat	9	19	72
	Is your current manual workload:		
	Too heavy or much too heavy	About right	Too light or much too light
All	36	58	6
BMW	19	72	9
GM	30	68	2
Fiat	61	29	10
	How much time do you have to do the work currently assigned to you?		
	Too much or far too much	About right	Too little or far too little
All	6	44	50
BMW	9	47	44
GM	6	54	40
Fiat	4	27	69
	Is your current work speed or work pace:		
	Too fast or much too fast	About right	Too slow or much too slow
All	54	45	1
BMW	43	54	3
GM	44	55	1
Fiat	79	21	0

felt they were generous), the majority believed they were under-staffed in their work areas. Although this is not surprising, given lean production's imperative of waste elimination, it does suggest that many workers did not endorse this principle (particularly at BMW), which is equally unsurprising. Understaffing was more apparent in relation to relief staff; overall, a greater number of workers indicated inadequate provision of relief staff to enable them to leave the line.

Significant numbers of workers also reported work overload. Respondents were asked whether their current manual workload, for example, positioning and fastening pieces, moving and lifting sub-assemblies and use of air tool torque, was too light, too heavy or about right. Over a third of workers felt that their workload was too heavy although the figure was much less at BMW but much greater – nearly two-thirds – at Fiat. An additional question used to measure workload intensity generated more negative patterns: 50 per cent of workers felt that they had too little time to complete their work assignments (nearly 70 per cent of Fiat workers indicated this). Similar proportions of workers in the British plants felt that their current work speed was too fast whilst nearly 80 per cent of Fiat workers indicated this.

These patterns were also mediated by age. On all three measures younger workers were more likely to report overload and excessive work speed compared to their older colleagues, especially in the direct worker group. One reason for this may be that whilst it took a relatively small amount of time to learn the task routines required for each job, it took much longer to become accustomed to the intensity and arduous nature of lean production work. This partly accounts for the contrast between the British and Italian plants where in the latter case the workforce was much younger and based in the rural South. Another factor is the effect of the traditions of informal seniority arrangements in British automotive production. Whilst seniority principles are not formally institutionalised in union agreements governing job classifications and labour deploy-ment as is the case in the USA (see for example, Milkman 1997), in the British case informal understandings between managers and unions mean that there is still a tendency for older workers to gravi-tate towards easier jobs (Danford, 1999; Jurgens *et al.*, 1993). These traditions had not taken hold at the greenfield Fiat plant.

Table 2.7   Workers' views on maintaining the pace of production (row percentages)

	For what part of each day do you work as fast as you can so you don't fall behind?			
	All day	**75% of the time**	**50% of the time**	**25% of the time or less**
All	28	21	19	32
BMW	34	13	24	29
GM	22	22	19	37
Fiat	30	29	14	28

	Could you work at the pace of your current job until the age of 60?			
	Yes	**Likely**	**Not likely**	**No**
All	13	15	24	48
BMW	20	15	20	45
GM	17	21	32	30
Fiat	0	6	17	77
Aged 18–30 yrs	3	10	20	67
Aged 31–40 yrs	11	15	29	46
Aged 41–50 yrs	16	16	22	45
Aged 51–65 yrs	39	22	13	26

Two additional questions explored the problem of work intensity further by asking respondents what proportion of each day they had to 'work as fast as you can' to keep up with the rhythm of production and whether they felt they could maintain their current work pace until the age of 60 (see Table 2.7). The results showed that overall, as many as two-thirds of employees had to work at full speed at least half the time to keep up with the pace of production; nearly half had to work at full speed for at least three quarters of the time. At BMW and Fiat around a third of workers indicated that they had to work at full speed for the whole day. Not surprisingly, nearly three-quarters felt that they would be unlikely to maintain the current pace of work until the age of 60; as many as 94 per cent of Fiat's relatively younger workers indicated this (and again, this result was partly a function of age in all three plants).

Quality of working life on the lean production line

The previous section provided a picture of a fairly extensive pattern of work intensity in each plant, a pattern which seems to contradict the 'working smarter not harder' mantra of lean production. However, we had a more pertinent issue for this research. For those who laboured on the assembly lines of these different lean production regimes was there a potential link between work intensity and health? There exists ample evidence that excessive workloads and effort intensification are likely to have a detrimental effect on employee welfare and stress at work (Anderson-Connolly *et al.*, 2002; Green, 2001; Macdonald, 2003). There is also evidence that insufficient job control – or lack of employee autonomy – can be a key mediator in this stress relationship since workers who are dissatisfied with the amount of influence they can exert over their working conditions are more likely to perceive work rates more negatively (Macdonald, 2003; Peterson, 2003).

The managerial rhetoric of lean production has consistently raised the prospect that the re-engineered assembly lines in the global automotive industry along with labour deployment strategies such as teamworking and multi-tasking are likely to increase the levels of workers' autonomy whilst reducing work intensity and stress. The questionnaire survey investigated these assumptions by adopting a series of measures of employee influence and workplace stress. Bivariate and multivariate statistical techniques were then used to explore associations between stress patterns and such factors as autonomy, workload and management-employee relations.

Employee autonomy

The extent of autonomy experienced by these workers was analysed along two dimensions. The first investigated a manifestation of direct management control of the labour process by considering the degree of managerial surveillance of work performance on the line. The second investigated employees' influence and control over their own work practices.

There is growing evidence that a high degree of management surveillance is an increasingly pervasive and powerful aspect of management control in British workplaces (for example, White *et al.*, 2004). The issue was explored by asking respondents how closely

Table 2.8   **Management surveillance (row percentages)**

	How closely is your work performance monitored by management?			
	Very closely	**Closely**	**Some**	**Not closely**
All	26	37	24	13
BMW	32	41	24	3
GM	33	39	21	7
Fiat	11	26	31	31
Direct	25	39	22	14
Indirect workers	28	33	31	8
Secure Workers	29	25	34	12
Insecure Workers	25	41	20	13
Bullied by managers	35	35	17	13
Rarely bullied	21	37	29	12

they felt their work performance was monitored by management. Table 2.8 shows a pattern of high surveillance although this was much stronger in the two British plants. At BMW and GM, over 70 per cent of workers felt that their work performance was monitored either very closely or closely by management whereas at Fiat this was lower at 37 per cent. As far as general patterns were concerned, there was little difference between direct assembly line workers and indirect workers. This suggests that surveillance was not just a result of the usual performance control protocols of the assembly line but instead a function of a more pervasive low-trust culture of management control. Closer monitoring was also felt by employees who were concerned about job security and those who had been subjected to bullying by their managers (both these variables are analysed in the next section).

The extent of employees' influence and control at work was operationalised by asking respondents how much influence they exerted over the way they carried out their work, how much they were able to vary the pace of their work over the course of the day, how much control they had for resolving problems that prevented them from doing their job, and how easy it was to change the things they did not like about their jobs. The results are shown in Table 2.9.

Table 2.9   Workers' views on job influence and autonomy (row percentages)

| | How much influence do you have over the way you do your job? | | | | |
	A great deal	A fair amount	Some	Very little	None at all
All	8	19	25	26	22
BMW	10	20	37	14	19
GM	10	22	22	31	15
Fiat	1	15	28	32	34

| | Over the course of a day, how much can you vary the pace of your work? | | | | |
	A great deal	A fair amount	Some	Very little	None at all
All	7	9	24	22	38
BMW	7	10	22	25	36
GM	9	6	23	18	44
Fiat	4	9	24	22	38

| | How much control do you have sorting out problems that prevent you from doing your job? | | | | |
	A great deal	A fair amount	Some	Very little	None at all
All	10	26	29	26	9
BMW	6	22	35	29	8
GM	17	22	23	28	9
Fiat	6	34	32	20	8

| | How easy is it for you to change the things you do not like about your job? | | | | |
	Very easy	Easy	Neither	Difficult	Very difficult
All	2	5	17	38	38
BMW	0	7	21	47	25
GM	1	5	19	40	35
Fiat	6	4	9	26	56

The first point to note is that there is little evidence here to support the conventional lean production analysis which places great emphasis upon the 're-skilling' and 'de-taylorisation' of the assembly line (Kenney and Florida, 1993; Womack *et al.*, 1990), or, as Adler put it, that blurring boundaries between the design and execution of production tasks raised the prospects for the emergence of a new 'democratic Taylorism' (1993: 98). There was a general pattern of relatively weak job control amongst these semi-skilled production line workers and unskilled labourers, far lower than is generally the case for skilled production workers (see for example Danford *et al.*, 2005). Only one third of respondents in the British plants felt they exerted either a great deal or a fair amount of influence over the way they carried out their work and only one in six felt the same at Fiat. Larger proportions of workers at GM and Fiat felt that they did have some control in resolving problems that prevented them from doing their jobs; this in part was a reflection of the total quality management practices in these plants. However, there was little evidence that this influence extended to the types of change and control that more obviously correspond with labour's interests. For example, large proportions of workers at all plants felt that they had little scope for varying the pace of their work and very large majorities indicated that it was difficult to change the facets of their jobs that they did not like.

A summative scale of employee autonomy was based on these four questions. Responses to each were coded from four (a great deal/very easy) to zero (none at all/very difficult). This group of questions had an internal consistency reliability (Cronbach's Alpha) of 0.621. The mean score results in Table 2.10 confirm that although worker autonomy was relatively higher in the British plants, the general pattern was low autonomy in all plants. Also, active union members tended to report higher autonomy than their less active colleagues as did workers who indicated feeling secure in their jobs compared to the more insecure. A much greater (and statistically significant) difference existed between direct (semi-skilled) and indirect (predominantly unskilled) production workers. In this case, whilst autonomy is normally associated with higher skill, the result is consistent with other differences between these two groups. That is, lack of employee influence seems to be more acute for those whose labour power is consumed directly on the tightly controlled lean production lines.

Table 2.10   Employee autonomy scale (0–16)

	Mean Score
BMW	6.16
GM	5.96
Fiat	5.38
Aged 18–30 yrs	5.70
Aged 31–40 yrs	5.58
Aged 41–50 yrs	6.03
Aged 51–65 yrs	6.28
Direct workers	5.42
Indirect workers	6.82
Active union members	5.95
Non-active union members	5.46
Secure workers	6.18
Insecure workers	5.61

Workplace stress

Research has shown that repetitive work of the type found on auto-mobile production lines is more likely to have a negative impact on employees' physical and psychological well-being. Notwithstanding the 'working smarter' claims of the proponents of lean production, this negative effect is often a function of work routines characterised by short cycle times and determined by production process time or speed of the assembly line (Macdonald, 2003). Our survey investigated this relationship by asking a number of questions about the more negative features of auto assembly work and workers' ability to cope with these. The first set of questions is shown in Table 2.11. Workers were asked how often over the previous month they had worked in physical pain or discomfort; what proportion of the typical working day they worked in physically awkward positions; what proportion of the working day could be described as boring or monotonous; and how often they had felt exhausted at the end of their shift in the previous month. The results suggested the existence of fairly extensive stressors. Around a third of workers in the British plants, and over 70 per cent of Italian workers at Fiat

Table 2.11   Workers' evaluation of work demands (row percentages)

	In the last month at work, how often have you worked with physical pain or discomfort?		
	Every day or most days	Half the time	A few days/never
All	34	11	55
BMW	23	4	73
GM	31	8	61
Fiat	50	21	28

	What part of each day do you work in physically awkward positions?		
	All to ¾ of the time	Half of the time	¼ of the time or less
All	28	13	59
BMW	18	8	74
GM	25	12	63
Fiat	43	20	37

	What part of each day would you describe your work as boring or monotonous?		
	All to ¾ of the time	Half of the time	¾ of the time or less
All	59	18	23
BMW	44	17	39
GM	61	20	19
Fiat	70	16	14

	In the last month, how often have you felt exhausted after your shift?		
	Every day or most days	Half the time	A few days or never
All	53	14	33
BMW	45	17	38
GM	52	13	35
Fiat	63	13	24

indicated working in pain or physical discomfort at least half the time. Exactly half of the Italian workers surveyed reported working in pain either every day or most days. This was despite the fact that the Fiat Melfi plant was the most recently constructed plant with more advanced production line technology (though not extensively roboticised). Large proportions of workers felt that much of their work was boring or monotonous; this was particularly the case at GM and Fiat. There were less inter-plant differences with regard reported feelings of exhaustion after each shift. To sum these patterns up, working 'harder' rather than 'smarter' seemed to be the common experience for a good two thirds of the workers surveyed.

As well as measuring employee experience of the physical demands of work on the line we investigated the more psycho-logical aspects of this, that is, questions concerning how workers coped with the demands of production. Respondents were asked whether they ever felt that 'things are getting on top of you during your shift', whether they felt 'tense and wound up' during the past month, and whether 'tiredness due to work restricted your parti-cipation in family and social activities'. The results are shown in Table 2.12. They suggest that workplace stress measured in this way was fairly widespread in the British plants but particularly prevalent in the Fiat plant. One reason for this contrast is that employees' average age and length of service were much lower in the Italian plant and stress problems are likely to be more pronounced amongst workers who are less accustomed to the to the physical demands of car assembly work. For example, 41 per cent of Fiat workers felt that things were getting on top of them during their shift a great deal or a fair amount compared to around a third of the workers in the British plants. Eighty six per cent of Fiat workers felt either very or somewhat tense and wound up at work during the previous month. A related question governs the link between work intensification, stress and the quality of life outside of work. As many as 79 per cent of Fiat workers felt that tiredness at work had restricted their participation in family and social activities at least half the time during the previous month (compared to around a half of BMW and GM workers). Moreover, 59 per cent of Fiat workers indicated that this was the case most days or every day.

Table 2.12   Workers' evaluation of the impact of work demands (row percentages)

| | *Do you ever feel that things are getting on top of you during your shift?* | | | | |
	A great deal	A fair amount	Some	Very little	None at all
All	16	19	36	18	11
BMW	15	15	36	21	13
GM	16	20	28	21	15
Fiat	18	23	46	10	3

| | *In the last month at work, how tense and wound up were you?* | | | |
	Very tense	Somewhat tense	Not very tense	Not tense at all
All	30	44	20	6
BMW	24	42	21	14
GM	18	41	21	20
Fiat	47	39	13	1

| | *In the last month, how often has tiredness due to work restricted your participation in family and social activities?* | | | | |
	Every day	Most days	Half the time	A few days	Never
All	15	27	14	30	14
BMW	19	20	10	26	25
GM	10	23	12	40	15
Fiat	19	40	20	20	1

The survey also operationalised an additional stress factor that might be expected to have a more acute effect on employees' sense of well-being: workplace bullying. Although managerial harassment in different forms has long been regarded as a typical feature of the process of direct management control of production workers it is only relatively recently that this has been problematised as an issue of concern in contemporary employment relations. The International Labour Organization defined bullying as a form of workplace violence in which a person is threatened or assaulted and that can originate in customers and co-workers at any level of the organisation. The

Table 2.13   Workers' experience of bullying at work (row percentages)

	Do you feel bullied at work?				
	A great deal	A fair amount	Some	Very little	Never
Bullied by a fellow worker	4	3	12	20	60
Bullied by a team leader	8	8	16	16	51
Bullied by a manager	17	12	17	21	33

	How closely is your work performance monitored by management?			
	Very closely	Closely	Some	Not closely
Bullied by a manager	35	35	17	13
Rarely or never bullied	21	37	29	13

	Do you ever feel that things are getting on top of you during your shift?				
	A great deal	A fair amount	Some	Very little	None at all
Bullied by a manager	24	24	34	9	8
Rarely or never bullied	9	18	36	22	15

	In the last month at work, how tense and wound up were you?			
	Very tense	Somewhat tense	Not very tense	Not tense at all
Bullied by a manager	45	47	7	1
Rarely or never bullied	16	47	28	9

survey asked respondents whether they had ever felt bullied by a fellow worker, or a team leader, or a manager. The results are shown in Table 2.13.

The results suggest that the experience of bullying by co-workers, including teamleaders, was experienced by a sizeable minority of workers. Overall, 19 per cent of workers had experienced bullying at least some of the time by co-workers and 32 per cent by teamleaders (again the position was worse in the Fiat plant). The data also show that nearly half the workers surveyed reported being bullied by their managers at least some of the time. There is nothing unusual in this statistic. Notwithstanding the currently fashionable interest in highlighting bullying and other features of the 'overwork culture' affecting professional and middle class workers (for example, Bunting, 2004), in recent decades workplace case studies have provided abundant evidence of managerial harassment of manual workers (for example, Beynon, 1984; Danford, 1999; Garrahan and Stewart, 1992; Nichols and Beynon, 1977; Roberts, 1993). An important question that arises, however, is the effect that such

Table 2.14   Workplace stress scale (0–15)

	Mean Score
BMW	7.68
GM	8.11
Fiat	9.60
Aged 18–30 yrs	9.28
Aged 31–40 yrs	8.05
Aged 41–50 yrs	8.39
Aged 51–65 yrs	7.38
Direct workers	8.75
Indirect workers	7.75
Active union members	8.79
Non-active union members	7.98
Bullied by manage	9.75
Rarely or never bullied	7.37
Workers closely monitored	8.63
Not closely monitored	8.19
Secure workers	8.66
Insecure workers	8.12
Workload too heavy	10.47
Workload about right/too light	7.40
Work speed too fast	9.90
Work speed about right/too slow	6.72

treatment might have on workers' sense of well-being and stress levels. Table 2.13 shows that there is a relationship between the experience of being bullied and managerial surveillance. There was also a closer relationship between the experience of being bullied and such stress indicators as whether 'things are getting on top of you' and feeling 'tense and wound up' at work.

Four of these questions were used to create a summative scale of workplace stress: 'in the last month how often have you worked with physical pain or discomfort'; 'how tense and wound up were you at work'; 'how often have you felt exhausted after your shift', and lastly; 'do you ever feel that things are getting on top of you during your shift'. This group of questions had an internal consistency reliability (Cronbach's Alpha) of 0.756.

The mean scores are shown in Table 2.14. These results confirm a significant difference between the British and the Italian plants. There were also significantly higher stress scores for younger workers and direct production workers, for workers who had experienced bullying from their managers, and for workers who felt that their workload was too heavy and work speed too fast.

Table 2.15   Correlations between selected workload/work environment and stress variables

	Physical pain	Exhausted	Things getting on top	Tense & wound up	Workplace stress scale
Work speed	0.358**	0.456**	0.353**	0.305**	0.476**
Workload	0.312**	0.395**	0.285**	0.195**	0.372**
Bullied by managers	0.267**	0.242**	0.258**	0.390**	0.337**
Work in a team	–0.190**	–0.112	–0.205**	–0.306**	–0.244**
Job insecurity	0.014	0.172**	0.082	0.060	0.072
High surveillance	–0.083	0.176**	0.079	0.054	0.061
Autonomy	–0.194**	–0.321**	–0.241**	–0.131	–0.281**
Management performance	–0.346**	–0.364**	–0.299**	–0.264**	–0.355**
Union performance	–0.095	–0.071	–0.071	–0.066	–0.061

*$p = 0.05$ ** $p = 0.01$

Our bivariate and multivariate analysis then investigated evidence of association between some of the workload/work environment variables and the different indicators of workplace stress. Bivariate correlation analysis (using Spearman's rho correlation tests) showed that each of our stress variables was associated with higher work speed, higher workload and managerial bullying (Table 2.15). There was little association with both high surveillance and job insecurity (the latter was based on a question that asked employees whether or not they were concerned about losing their jobs in the next three years). The results also showed significant associations between lower stress scores and variables that reflected 'high performance' lean work practices – teamworking, employee autonomy and the management performance scale.

Finally, multivariate regression analysis was carried out on the stress scale to investigate the significance of these intervening variables along with worker attribute control variables. The dependent variable and two independent variables (autonomy and management performance scales) were all treated as interval level variables since they were regarded as sufficiently analogous to a genuine interval variable. Age and length of service were also interval level variables. The remainder were recoded dummies. We add the caveat that due to the relatively small size of the sample we present this as exploratory analysis only with the purpose of generating hypotheses for further research.

The model is presented in Table 2.16. This shows that once the controls are added and other potentially intervening effects taken into consideration, the 'high performance' variables of teamworking, employee autonomy and management performance together had no significant effect on the stress scale. Neither did job insecurity or management surveillance. The three variables that were positively related to worker stress were managerial bullying, excessive speed of work and excessive workload. Given the bulk of research that has highlighted the salience of such 'stressors' as speed of the assembly line and other production process drivers (Macdonald, 2003) this result does seem predictable. Nevertheless, it serves to remind us that the so-called 'empowerment' dimensions of lean production, such as increasing employee autonomy and participation, may matter little for the quality of working life on the shop floor. What does count is the negative impact of the lean imperative to drive labour ever harder.

Table 2.16   Regression of workplace stress scale on plant, workload and other work environment determinants

	Stress Scale	
	Unstandardised B coefficients	Significance
Constant	3.977	–
BMW	0.459	–
Fiat	0.907	–
Male/Female	0.106	–
Age	0.064	–
Length of service	–0.003	–
Direct/Indirect	0.242	–
Active in Union/Not Active	0.802	–
Teamworkers	–0.087	–
Speed of work	1.753	0.01
Workload	1.995	0.01
Bullied by managers	1.430	0.05
Job insecurity	0.614	–
Management surveillance	0.464	–
Autonomy	–0.029	–
Management performance	–0.141	–
Union performance	0.125	–

Adjusted R^2 = 0.367
N = 244

Conclusion

The global automotive industry constituted the empirical base of Womack *et al.*'s (1990) highly influential and polemical account of lean production. Its core thesis was that Western manufacturers could compete with the Japanese by putting into operation a set of high productivity managerial techniques and employee-centred processes that had universal application. In the 18 years that have passed since its publication the research has remained the reference point for the plethora of consultancy interventions and related management tool-kits centred on the re-organisation of plant and labour in different manufacturing capitals. As the opening chapters of this book have noted, the many advocates of lean production have mobilised their arguments for change by recourse to an ideology of 'one best way' and a belief that the specific practices and processes of lean offer workers the option of breaking the chains of Taylorism by providing new systems and environments of worker participation in continuous improvement. This is Womack *et al.*'s so-called 'creative tension' in which workers are empowered to address and engage with the technical challenges of producing commodities on a mass scale.

In this chapter, we have investigated the realities of worker experience of lean through employee samples at three distinctive case studies. The first, BMW-Cowley, constituted an example of a brownfield plant re-engineered through investments in new mass production technologies and new, cooperative approaches to the management of the employment relationship. The second, GM-Vauxhall, was a more conventional brownfield plant where the introduction of lean manufacturing techniques had been more gradualist and subject to a degree of union and rank and file contestation. The third, Fiat, stood out as a greenfield, rural site that by the time of the research had matured into a 15-year-old plant where the original implementation of complete just-in-time manufacturing processes and technologies – along with supportive partnership institutions – had become well embedded. In many respects, the Fiat case constituted the lean ideal type (at least in technological terms).

Our results showed that the quality of working life and condition of labour on the three production lines were not quite what the advocates of lean, who tend to describe these things from a distance, might have anticipated. On the other hand, the results also suggest that for those who actually implement their capital accumulation strategies based on lean doctrine and process, that is the automotive employers, the results might seem more satisfying.

Two main patterns of worker experience were apparent. The first concerned management and union style. We found that workers in each plant hardly gave their manager's performance a ringing endorsement in the areas of consultation and respect. Significant numbers in the sample highlighted a considerable gap between the managerial discourse of respect (through cooperation and partnership in shop-floor social relations) and actual worker experience. Notably, this was particularly the case at Fiat's Melfi plant where, nearly 15 years after the company completed the large scale recruitment of young, malleable, rural workers displaying the 'correct attitudes' to industry and labour, the workforce sample seemed more oppositionalist to management and union partnership than the two British groups. The second concerned the condition of labour on the line. Our data provided clear indicators of labour intensification with a deleterious impact upon employee welfare and health. For example, large proportions of workers, and more so in Fiat's model lean plant, signalled experiences of working in physical pain, working in awkward positions, feeling exhausted at the end of a day's shift (and one marked by boredom and monotony). There was little evidence of even a modicum of meaningful employee discretion and autonomy. In short, our data exposed widespread rank and file experience of a more intensive and arduous life on the line and one that does not quite resonate with Womack *et al.*'s (1990) notion of 'creative tension'. Equally worryingly, these material factors, along with some evidence of managerial bullying, contributed to the relatively high levels of stress suffered by these workers.

Of course, we offer the caveat that our samples were small in each plant (though the shop stewards were careful to ensure that all core direct and indirect job roles were adequately represented in the sampling procedure). Nevertheless, our results do correspond with many of the critical labour process studies that have attempted to interrogate the claims of lean production by regarding the experience of labour as a prime – rather than secondary – consideration (for example, Danford, 1999; Delbridge, 1998; Elger and Smith, 2006; Garrahan and Stewart, 1992; Graham, 1995; Nichols and Sugur, 2004; Rinehart *et al.*, 1997). What these studies, and the data presented in this chapter, remind us is that the technological accounts of lean production, accounts that have become so dominant in the business literature, merely serve to obscure the unalterable underlying capitalist dynamic that shapes advanced systems for mass producing commodities. That is, lean manufacturing should be viewed quite properly as merely the latest version of a mass production paradigm that brings together technology and process to secure what Marx (1976: 533) termed, 'the inversion of extensive magnitude into intensive magnitude, or magnitude of degree'. In other words, the compression of a greater mass of labour into a given period. Many critical labour process studies of lean production have noted this. What we have tried to highlight is that, in the context of declining labour standards and union influence at work, closing up the porosity of the working day in these advanced automotive plants is a constant factor that continues to impair the health and well-being of those whose labour power is directly consumed on the lean assembly line.

References

Adler, P. (1993) 'Time and Motion Regained', *Harvard Business Review*, January–February: 97–108.

Anderson-Connolly, R. Grunberg, L. Greenberg, E. and Moore, S. (2002) 'Is lean mean? Workplace transformation and employee well-being, *Work, Employment and Society*, 16(3): 389–413.

Arrowsmith, J. (2002) 'Pacts for employment and competitiveness: GM Vauxhall Motors', *European Foundation for the Improvement of Living and Working Conditions*.

Beynon, H. (1984) Working for Ford, Second Edition. Harmondsworth: Penguin.

Bunting, M. (2004) *Willing Slaves. How the Overwork Culture is Ruling Our Lives*. London: HarperCollins.

Camuffo, A. and Volpato, G. (1998) 'Making manufacturing lean in the Italian automobile industry: The trajectory of Fiat' in M. Freyssenet, A. Mair, K. Shimizu and G. Volpato (eds) *One Best Way? Trajectories and industrial models of the world's automobile producers*, OUP.

Coupar, W. and Stevens, B. (1998) 'Towards a new model of partnership. Beyond the "HRM versus industrial relations" argument' in Sparrow, P. and Marchington, M. (eds) *Human Resource Management. The New Agenda*. London: FT Pitman Publishing.

Danford, A. (1999) *Japanese Management Techniques and British Workers*. London: Routledge.

Danford, A., Richardson, M., Stewart, P., Tailby, S. and Upchurch, M. (2007) 'Capital Mobility, Job Loss and Union Strategy: The Case of the UK Aerospace Industry', *Labor Studies Journal*, 32(3): 298–318.

Danford, A., Richardson, M., Stewart, P., Tailby, S. and Upchurch, M. (2005) *Partnership and the High Performance Workplace. Work and Employment Relations in the Aerospace Industry*. Basingstoke: Palgrave Macmillan.

Delbridge, R. (1998) *Life on the Line in Contemporary Manufacturing*, Oxford: Oxford University Press.

Eckardt, A. and Klemm, M. (2003) 'The internationalization of a premium automobile producer: The BMW Group and the case of Rover' in M. Freyssenet, K. Shimizu and G. Volpato (eds) *Globalization or Regionalization of the European Car Industry?*, Palgrave (in association with *GERPISA*).

Elger, T. and Smith, C. (2005) *Assembling Work. Remaking Factory Regimes in Japanese Multinationals in Britain*. Oxford: Oxford University Press.

Gallie, D., Felstead, A. and Green, F. (2001) 'Employer Policies and Organizational Commitment in Britain 1992–1997, *Journal of Management Studies*, 38(8): 1081–101.

Garrahan, P. and Stewart, P. (1992) *The Nissan Enigma: Flexibility at Work in a Local Economy*. London: Mansell.

Graham, L. (1995) *On the Line at Subaru-Isuzu: The Japanese Model and the American Worker*. Ithaca, New York: ILR Press.

Green, F. (2001) 'It's Been A Hard Day's Night: The Concentration and Intensification of Work in Late Twentieth Century Britain', *British Journal of Industrial Relations*, 39(1): 53–80.

Heery, E. (2002) 'Partnership versus organising: alternative futures for British trade unionism', *Industrial Relations Journal*, 33(1): 20–35.

Hodson, R. (2001) *Dignity at Work*. Cambridge: Cambridge University Press.

Jurgens, U., Malsch, M. and Dohse, K. (1993) *Breaking From Taylorism: Changing Forms of Work in the Automobile Industry*. Cambridge: Cambridge University Press.

Kelly, J. (2004) 'Social Partnership Agreements in Britain: Labor Cooperation and Compliance', *Industrial Relations*, 43(1): 267–92.

Kenney, M. and Florida, R. (1993) Beyond Mass Production: The Japanese System and its Transfer to the U.S. Oxford: Oxford University Press.

Lanzara, G.F. and Patriotta, G. (2007) 'The institutionalization of knowledge in an automotive factory: templates, inscriptions and the problem of durability', *Organizational Studies Online First*, January 2007.

Macdonald, W. (2003) 'Work Demands and Stress in Repetitive Blue-Collar Work' in Peterson, C. (ed.) *Work Stress. Studies of the Context, Content and Outcomes of Stress*. New York: Baywood Publishing Company Inc.

MacDuffie, J.P. and Pil, F.K. (1999) 'What Makes Transplants Thrive: Managing the Transplant of "Best Practice" at Japanese Auto Plants in North America', *Journal of World Business*, 4: 372–92.

MacDuffie, J.P. (1995) 'Human resource Bundles and Manufacturing Performance: Organizational Logic and Flexible Production Systems in the World Auto Industry', *Industrial and Labor Relations Review*, 48(2): 199–221.

Marx, K. (1976) *Capital. A Critique of Political Economy*. London: Penguin Books.

Mayhew, C. (2003) 'Exploration of the Links between Workplace Stress and Precarious Employment' in Peterson, C. (ed.) *Work Stress. Studies of the Context, Content and Outcomes of Stress*. New York: Baywood Publishing Company Inc.

Milkman, R. (1997) *Farewell to the Factory. Auto Workers in the Late Twentieth Century*. Berkeley: University of California Press.

Nichols, T. and Beynon, H. (1977) *Living with Capitalism: Class Relations and the Modern Factory*. London: Routledge and Kegan Paul.

Nichols, T. and Sugur, N. (2004) *Global Management, Local Labour: Turkish Workers and Modern Industry*. Basingstoke: Palgrave Macmillan.

Patriotta, G. and Lanzara, G.F. (2006) 'Identity, Institutions, and New Work Roles: The case of a green field automotive factory' in *American Behavioral Scientist*, vol. 49, no. 7, pp. 987–98.

Peterson, C. (2003) 'Workplace Changes in Australia and their Effects on Stress', in Peterson, C. (ed.) *Work Stress. Studies of the Context, Content and Outcomes of Stress*. New York: Baywood Publishing Company Inc.

Pulignano, V. (2002a) 'Just-in-time and social relations in the auto-component industry' in Actes du GERPISA International Network no. 33.

Pulignano, V. (2002b) 'Restructuring of work and union representation: A developing framework for workplace industrial relations in Britain and Italy', *Capital & Class*, Spring 2002.

Rinehart, J., Huxley, C. and Robertson, D. (1997) *Just Another Car Factory? Lean Production and its Discontents*. Ithaca and London: ILR Press.

Roberts, I. (1993) *Craft, Class and Control: The Sociology of a Shipbuilding Community*. Edinburgh: Edinburgh University Press.

Stewart, P. (1997) 'Striking smarter and harder at Vauxhall: The new industrial relations of lean production?, *Capital & Class*, Spring 1997.

Tuckman, A. and Whittall, M. (2006) 'As a phoenix risen? Union organisation, Rover cars and the British motor industry' in G. Gall (ed.) *Union Recognition: Organising and bargaining outcomes*. Routledge.

White, M., Hill, S., Mills, C. and Smeaton, D. (2004) *Managing to Change? British Workplaces and the Future of Work*. Basingstoke: Palgrave Macmillan.

Womack, J.P., Jones, D.T. and Roos, D. (1990) *The Machine that Changed the World: The triumph of lean production*. New York: Rawson Macmillan.

3
Lean Production: The Original Myth Reconsidered

Dan Coffey and Carole Thornley

Introduction

This chapter commences with a reassessment of the data which originally emboldened leading figures in an MIT-headquartered car assembly plant productivity survey, conducted in the late 1980s, to declare that definitive evidence had been collated to show conclusive organisational advantages in production centred in Japan, which for successfully emulating firms abroad would dramatically lower the hours of assembly plant labour required to make cars at any level of factory automation. 'Lean production' – a Western made term – was invented and promoted in this connection, giving rise to an enormous subsequent literature, both prescriptive and critical. The practices of one car producer in particular, Toyota, were identified as the key to success by the apostles of lean production – the reference point for lean thinking. An alternative interpretive reading of the original survey data is first advanced, pointing to quite different conclusions which could have been drawn had the survey authors been more open to other possibilities, and which helps explain why the radical worldwide lift in production potentials predicted by lean thinkers has not transpired. We next consider the relevance of our interpretive reading for the understanding of labour process issues, noting a striking anomaly in the Japanese variety of industrial capitalism when compared with the West. We consider in this connection another view too of ongoing workplace experiments in the organisation of assembly processes at Toyota – quite distinct from the lean literature.

The subsidiary theme of this chapter is industrial crisis, and the contexts thereby provided to the career launch of lean production. Two are relevant. First, the idea of lean production was launched into a space opened up by a particular kind of industrial crisis in the West, a complex one no doubt and the scale of which should not be exaggerated, but a crisis nonetheless as Western firms in the auto and other sectors struggled to cope with Japanese encroachments on market territories. This provided a context conducive to popular acceptance of bold claims about Japanese manufacturing prowess. Second, shortly thereafter the Japanese industrial economy entered a deep recession; but while the reputation of Japan's national economic model has crumbled in the West, Toyota remains a reference point (for many) as the harbinger and embodiment of 'lean production'. We embed our opening discussion in the first crisis, before touching on the second.

Lean production: an original myth revisited

To progress as planned, let us first reconsider the foundations of lean production, as regards both the coining of the phrase and what it was invented to convey.

The IMPV productivity survey

The words lean production were coined in connection with a worldwide survey of car assembly plant productivity conducted at the close of the 1980s as part of the International Motor Vehicle Programme (IMVP) headquartered at MIT, in the US. The chief architect of the assembly plant survey, the engineer J.F. Krafcik, invented the phrase after some earlier efforts ('fragile production') proved inadequate to purpose. The exercise was funded to a considerable degree by the auto industry itself. Publicity for the survey's purported findings, and the career launch of lean production, came with the best-selling Womack *et al.* (1990), *The Machine That Changed The World*. Both in this original book, and subsequently, Toyota has been highlighted as the key firm for other producers seeking to adopt 'lean thinking' (Womack and Jones, 2003). There has been a tendency for some critics since to dismiss the MIT survey peremptorily, but a better approach is to look closely at its construction and to take its findings seriously. The quality of access enjoyed by the project to the world's car assembly sites – amounting to what Womack *et al.* (*ibid.*: 75–6) estimate at about half world manufacturing capacity at the time, with information obtained from more than 90 car assembly plants – mean that if any systematic patterns can be discerned in the data, they are worth considering. And as we shall note, these suggest points of interest quite different from the inferences drawn and heavily promoted in Womack *et al.*, and in subsequent or related publications. Prior attention to context is important, and before developing this point we should first pause to take stock of this context and to properly locate our own re-interpretation.

Lean production was launched as a literary venture in the context of the dislocations of the 1980s. By the end of this decade foreign direct investment by Japanese car assemblers in Western countries was substantial: Honda, Nissan and Toyota had opened both car assembly sites and engine plants in the US, Mazda an assembly site, and a number of collaborative ventures were under way with indigenous American firms including Chrysler and Mitsubishi at Diamond Star, and GM and Toyota at NUMMI; Europe had also experienced a surge in Japanese investment and involvement.[1] Coming on the back of large Japanese surpluses in trade in cars which had built up from the 1970s, the period was one uneasily poised between trauma and relief for some at least of the stake-holders in the Western auto sectors. Lean production was actively promoted as indicating the advantages to Western interests of engagement in this process. This proposition is practically the *leitmotif* of Womack *et al.* (1990), and it runs throughout the discussion of the IMVP productivity survey (see *ibid.*: 76–7, 84, 87–8).

The asserted connection between gaining access to lean production and engaging with Japanese car makers was quickly taken up: lean production became a 'major' stated gain from Japanese foreign direct investment (and collaboration). The distinguished Robert Gilpin, Eisenhower Professor (Emeritus) of Public and International Affairs at the University of Princeton, in a majestic survey of the challenges of global capitalism, notes how the appeal to lean production has come to inform policy debate on the extent of positive spin-offs from foreign direct investment (FDI) activities:

> FDI can create externalities, spin-offs or spillovers that confer bene-
> fits on the host economy over and above the strictly economic

benefits of trade ... It is frequently pointed out, for example, that the American and British economies have greatly benefited from the high levels of Japanese investment in their economies; this FDI has encouraged firms in both countries to adopt Japanese 'lean production techniques' and to increase product quality. (Gilpin, 2000: 175)

At the same time, consideration of this passage helps locate our own contribution in this chapter. Lean production was a phrase invented to describe a big claim about comparative resource productivity in a factory process. By dint of its attachment to Japanese car assemblers, it has since become the favoured umbrella term for panoplies of individual management techniques associated (rightly or wrongly) with these firms, and especially Toyota. Research into individual practices is in no way vitiated by a critique of the foundation of lean production in the IMVP world survey, and our contra-position in this section does not imply that findings would lack substance or interest.[2] But the global authority provided these practices, by the invention of lean production as an invocation of the productivity benefits which the survey's authors claimed to see in their data, is a phenomenon in its own right: it is this authority which we challenge.

The most striking claim to emerge from the IMVP survey was that compelling evidence had been uncovered of a rather massive labour productivity differential between car assembly plants clustered in Japan and those based elsewhere, partial exceptions being transplants operated by Japanese firms or plants adopting Japanese practices. The labour productivity measure employed was based on a calculation of the hours of plant labour used to undertake a pre-specified set of car-assembly tasks, completion of the full set of tasks by the relevant workers being indicated by the production of a finished car. It was maintained that the differences observed in plant level labour productivity could not be adequately accounted for by differences in process automation. On this basis, world regions were ranked as being more or less efficient depending on the averaged values of their scores on the productivity index (regardless of automation): the average in Japan was 16.8 hours; Japanese transplants in North America 20.9 hours; US plants in North America 24.9 hours; and so forth – to encompass Japanese and US plants in

Europe, European plants in Europe, and the NICs (Womack *et al.*, 1990: 85).[3] Within each region the most (labour) productive site was also declared to be most efficient, the least productive least efficient, 'benchmarking' the best and worst.

What seems indisputable is that Japanese car plants achieved consistently 'good' scores on the index employed in the survey to measure labour productivity. An impressive score on a productivity measure may, of course, reflect the design of the measure. But even before coming to this point, it is also the case that Japanese sites were reported as more automated in relative terms, as noted in Womack *et al.* (*ibid.*: 94–5). The coincidence of an apparently high labour productivity with high automation means that one has to be convinced of the grounds for discounting the effects on the former of the latter, before accepting any type of efficiency ranking based solely on the labour index. Since such a discounting is integral to the position set out in Womack *et al.*, and since 'lean production' was invented in this context – how convincing was this part of the analysis?

An alternative reading

The answer is, not very. A scatter of observations on labour productivity and automation was presented in Womack *et al.* (*ibid.*: 94–5) for the worldwide sample of participating car plants, pooled together. Consider Figure 3.1, a visual aid to assist in describing key features of this data and its analysis. If we think of the plane of this figure as containing the scatter of observations obtained by the IMVP survey for its plant-level labour productivity and assembly process automation variables, then what was uncovered was that Japanese factories clustered in its bottom right hand corner – area J. Since the labour productivity index used was based on a calculation of the hours of labour required to perform a specified set of assembly tasks, a 'low' score was a 'good' score. The statistical procedure used in Womack *et al.* (*ibid.*) consisted of nothing more complex than a simple regression of this productivity index against measured automation (a higher value of the automation index implying greater process investment). On the grounds that despite having a statistically significant effect on labour productivity the sample variation in automation could only account for (*circa*) one-third of the variation in productivity, it was concluded that 'other' factors were

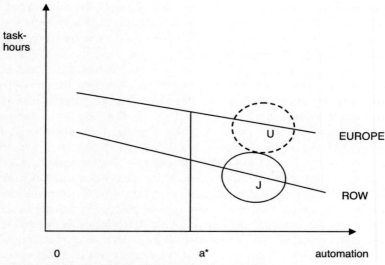

Figure 3.1   IMVP survey analysis – a stylised critique
Source: Developed from Coffey and Thornley (2006a)

more important. The productivity scores *per se* of Japanese sites then sustained the notion of competitive advantage.

But alternative readings were not pursued. For example, another point to emerge with considerable clarity from the scatter of observations was that factories in Europe scored consistently and particularly 'badly' on labour productivity against other sites at every level of assembly process automation – that is, against the rest of the world (ROW). Had the IMVP survey authors run with this feature of the data, some quite different inferences could have been drawn from those giving birth to 'lean production'. Their data suggests that a regression line for plants in Europe would have differed markedly in both intercept and coefficient from a separate regression line for plants elsewhere. With the best-fitting line for observations in the second category passing through rather than (largely) above the Japanese cluster, it would have been far harder had the data been divided in this way to make a case for Japanese exceptionalism *other* than for extremely high levels of automation relative to other plants outside of Europe. For its part, Europe would have been distinguished as a region not only by a productivity deficit at all levels of automation, but one growing seemingly worse at higher levels of automation.[4]

The changed perspective this entails of what distinguished Japanese sites in the survey is compounded by a second, somewhat overlooked, feature of the data. Of the observations for Europe-based sites displayed in the IMVP survey scatter, a considerable number were actually for plants owned and managed by American and Japanese firms. In fact between five and nine of the 18 sites displayed for Europe in the scatter were transplants to Europe. It is impossible to be precise as to the number – a quirk in Womack et al.[5] – but it begs the question as to whether some of the 'weak' sites in Europe were Japanese. In particular, what were the countries of origin for those sites in Europe displaying particularly high levels of assembly process automation – shown as region U in Figure 3.1.[6]

The manner in which the thesis of a new 'lean production' centred in Japan was extruded from the IMVP survey data was tendentious, if we put it no more strongly than that. But there is a third major objection to add to these first two, of equal importance.

This concerns the IMVP labour productivity index. While a full discussion goes beyond the scope of this chapter, Coffey (2006) demonstrates a major bias factor. As noted above, production of a finished car was used to proxy the completion by relevant workers of a full-set of pre-specified car assembly tasks; the output measure in fact used in calculating the productivity index was a full (24 hour) average day's production. But at the same time, the headcount of workers identified as being relevant to the performance of these tasks was multiplied by the length of a single standard non-overtime shift (net of breaks and other stoppages) – with each employee assumed to work only a single non-overtime shift in an average day for that site. Consequently, individual worker hours expended in excess of a single non-overtime shift were *not* included. Thus plants allocating or requiring significant overtime (paid or unpaid) would have experienced a definite 'advantage' in the productivity calculation. The question naturally arises as to whether the resulting pattern of advantages (and disadvantages) would have taken a form likely to effect systematic regional or national biases – that might still allow some useful comparative information to be drawn from the exercise. While the proximate determinants of the working day are manifold, it is reasonable enough to suppose that workloads in excess of a non-overtime shift will reflect

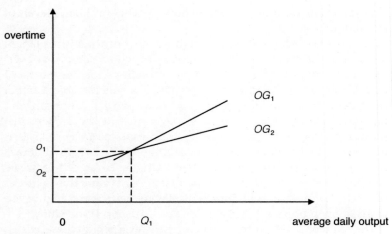

Figure 3.2   Overtime growth curves

both (i) normal working practices with regard to hours and (ii) the recent growth trajectory of productions.

Consider, for example, Figure 3.2. Imagine a site commencing from a position where it is currently producing an average (total) daily output of Q_1 units: reflecting current working practices employees score an average of o_1 hours of overtime. If product demand proved buoyant at plant level, and required an increase in production, part of the burden of adjustment may well be met by an increase in hours. If not anticipated, or of uncertain duration, the change could be steep, displayed (say) in an overtime-growth curve like curve OG_1; in the longer term plant managers could prefer to take on more workers rather than adjust heavily via overtime, implying a rather flatter overtime-growth curve, like curve OG_2. The precise trajectories both in the shorter run and longer run would reflect 'normal' working practices for the plant, and in turn could impact on what is perceived to be normal by plant managers and workforce. Another site commencing from the same point (an average daily output of Q_1 units) may have quite different initial overtime arrangements, commencing say with o_2 hours of overtime, and react differently to the effects of a change in demand. The effect of a reduction in production would exert a contrary movement (not necessarily symmetric) in the opposite direction.

While a cross-section study, there is clearly no *a priori* reason
to suppose that there were no systematic variations in growth trajectories and working practices across the sites which participated
in the IMVP survey. An interesting question is whether this sheds
light on the differential performance of sites in Europe (and remem-
bering that these sites included plants managed by non-European
transnationals). But there is also the question of how this could
have impacted elsewhere. Suppose one were to ask which of the
factories surveyed by the IMVP in 1989 and based outside of Europe
were likely to be particularly characterised by recently high growth
trajectories and long working hours: one hardly needs to be ima-
ginative to answer – Japanese sites. The boom in production in
this period for Japanese plants (especially in Japan) was exceptional,
while insofar as working practices go, overtime was proverbial
(see Kawahara, 1998: 237; Kenney and Florida, 1993: 264; also,
for a discussion of the Takaoka site in 1988, Williams, 1994: 211).
While a measurement error based on omitted overtime is a serious
one – rendering plant by plant comparisons invidious – one might
guess that Japan did not suffer.

The anomalies of Japan: the reorganisation of work at Toyota

It is worthwhile to pursue these points further, because what this
reading of the data suggests is by no means simple, and to stop at
this point would be a mistake.

Mean lean

Consider what is known about the working day (and year) in
Japan's manufacturing sectors. Here we might quote David Coates
reporting on the results of a government survey published a few
years after the IMVP survey:

> [W]hat other advanced capitalist economy needs (or indeed pos-
> sesses, as Japan does) a National Defense Council for Victims of
> *Karoshi* (death through overwork) ... in what other advanced cap-
> italist economy could a government survey (in 1992) report than
> one in six male manufacturing employees then worked more
> than 3,100 hours annually, and add that to work more than

3,000 hours (or 60 hours a week) was potentially lethal (Coates, 2000: 131).

Consider the probability that the high relative levels of automation in factory processes uncovered in the IMVP survey for the Japanese car industry combined with an extremely long working week for employees working within that industry. A moment's thought establishes the anomaly. Since Marx one is accustomed to think of investment in labour-displacing equipment as being associated with forms of production based on the extraction of a relative surplus, compatible of course with a shortening of the working day for wage earners. For Marx, the transition from manufacture to 'machino-facture' was an essential step forward in the long-term viability of capitalism: a system of production based on a mere summation of individual labours and an extension of the working day had become a threat to progress – hence the role of large manufacturers combining against the small to support 19th century British factory legislation. But investment in labour-displacing machinery, in the country upon which Marx based his analysis of industrial capitalism, was associated historically with extraction of a relative surplus that superceded earlier reliance on an extended working day. What is striking about the above description of Japan's auto industry is the coincidence in time and space of a displacement of workers in a production process by automation to a greater degree than evidenced for other mature capitalisms, but with a far longer working day.[7]

Our alternative reading of the data provided by the IMVP survey points to a hypothesis that can be used to frame further study of this point. On an hour by hour basis, were Japanese car plants actually struggling to convert labour time into finished products, a difficulty masked by high capital investment and a biased productivity measure?

This possibility is of considerable relevance to centre-left critics of firms like Toyota, who have identified in the workplaces of Japan a uniquely effective form of surplus extraction. To take an articulate example, Moody (1997) identifies lean production in the auto industry with a global assault on the conditions and experience of work – entailing for auto industry workers 'faster and harder work' (*ibid.*: 92). One appeal to managers of the rhetoric of a lean revolution could of course be that it helps push changes which do have the effect of undermining working conditions, but are in any case deemed advisable, desirable or necessary because they also help cut cost. And the precise content and context of such changes can only be investigated through direct study.[8] But while employees in the plant sites surveyed by the IMVP in Japan may well have experienced their work as both long and hard, the data collated by the survey which gave birth to the words lean production does not provide support for a thesis predicated on successful surplus extraction via work *intensification* – measured by *hourly* results. This does not, of course, preclude efforts to maintain work-rates at an as high as possible level given the constraints of worker responses to those efforts, and physical exhaustion. But the panoplies of management techniques identified with Japan's car firms in this survey are not associated (convincingly) with extra output per timed-labour input.

More specifically, the data points (tentatively) to possible limits in a system predicated on what, from the viewpoint of Western historical trajectories, would be an anomalous perseverance of an extreme working day with extensive factory automation. While demanding further research, car plants in Japan may actually have been encountering difficulties at the time of the IMVP survey. This contention is supported by a different kind of evidence, and from the lean thinker's lean firm, Toyota.

The Toyota assembly process experiments

Consider the fact that shortly after the IMVP survey was conducted Toyota began to experiment with a re-organisation of some of its assembly processes in Japan. In particular, it initiated experiments in line-segmentation, in which a conventional assembly line with a substantial manual component is sub-divided into linearly sequenced 'mini-lines', each connected by in-process buffers: Monden (1998) provides the best description by a writer with access to Toyota factories. The experiments grew out of the 'bubble period' in the Japanese economy – they commenced in the early 1990s – with Toyota admitting to having experienced problems with recruiting and retaining workers during the boom. It has publicised its experiments (still ongoing: see Benders and Morita, 2004) since as being intended to improve the workplace. But it is interesting to see, that in addition to recruitment and retention, Monden (*ibid.*: 357–62) tacitly adds a further reason: Toyota was also seeking a new approach to deal with cumulative problems experienced with stoppages on its conventional lines.

So far as the operations aspects of a conventionally arranged assembly line are concerned, the key point is that production is *synchronous*: a stop at any point on the line implies a simultaneous stop for the line as a whole. But were the assembly processes sub-divided into a sequence of mini-lines, a stop at any point can in principle be isolated, provided that the stoppage frequency is kept within limits. Workers on the afflicted segment can deal with the problem while production on adjacent segments continues unaffected – provided that the problem is dealt with quickly. The same workers would then have to increase their production pace to make good the lost time spent dealing with the problem, to 'rebalance' adjacent buffers. Production is *asynchronous*.

It is interesting that Monden attempts to reconcile asynchronicity with the notion that Toyota adheres to a just-in-time (JIT) manufacturing philosophy. He argues that what is important is not the elimination (as commonly supposed) of physical production stocks, but rather the reduction of *throughput times* (the sum total of the processing and handling times for items constituting work-in-progress). Since a segmented line which employs in-process buffers may do better than a conventional line in keeping down throughput times, Monden argues that there is no necessary contradiction between the Toyota experiments with segmented assembly and a just-in-time imperative. But he also goes one stage further, and claims that real reductions were in fact achieved.

But this in turn implies a claim that Toyota was experiencing quite significant problems with line stoppages, for the following reason. All else being equal, a segmented assembly line may operate with a throughput time which is lower than that on a conventional line, but only if the stoppage rate on the latter passes a minimum threshold frequency. If we denote this threshold stoppage rate by p^* and throughput times respectively on segmented and conventional lines by TS and TC, then only if the threshold probability of a stoppage on a conventional line exceeds p^* will TS be less than TC. Importantly, while the stoppage rate would have to exceed the threshold minimum, stoppages would still have to be bounded so as not to swamp even the buffered system. In concrete terms, therefore, we would be envisaging a 'real' stoppage problem, but within bounds.

It so happens that, based on the data presented by Monden and others for Toyota's experiments, we can give some idea of what sort of stoppage rates are implied. For it to be true that Toyota was enabled to *improve* its throughput times in its experiments with line segmentation and in-process buffers (the Monden thesis), then it must have expected stoppages in a conventional arrangement to be between more than 17 stops, or more than 85 stops, on average, in the production of each completed car. A range of imputed values could obviously be generated by changing some of the relevant parameters – but the actual size of the imputation is obviously less important than the issue raised.[9]

What could it mean?

It is interesting to note that Womack and Jones (2003), a follow up to Womack *et al.* (1990) intended as a reader's guide to lean thinking, is silent on the Toyota experiments (indeed, the entire thrust of their book is based on an assertion that Toyota production is synchronous). We can perhaps see why, by referring to Table 3.1. There is a Hobson's choice: there is either evidence that Toyota is *not* so preoccupied after all with manufacturing throughput times – the relevant case where stoppages are not generally a problem, but it segments its lines anyway – or Toyota *has* in fact experienced difficulties with stoppages, in which case it is still possible to argue (as with Monden) that Toyota really does take throughput times seriously. This, however, is only one point to note, and not the main one. The Toyota experiments commenced shortly after the IMVP

Table 3.1 A simple assembly model classification – stoppages and throughput times

	conventional assembly (synchronous)	segmented assembly (asynchronous)
localized stoppages = 0	**throughput gain** (relative to segmented)	throughput loss (relative to conventional)
localized stoppages > p^* (and bounded above)	throughput loss (relative to segmented)	**throughput gain** (relative to conventional)

survey, but reflected conditions prevailing at the time of the survey: if Monden is correct, we have further evidence of a manufacturing system under stress, *circa* the late 1980s.

Japan's industrial crisis and lean production

At this closing juncture some words may be desirable on the relationship between the phenomenon of lean production and industrial crises. The first crisis of note was an essentially Western one, which we have already discussed as informing the context in which Womack *et al.* (1990) gave public birth to lean production: of relevance here is the close association drawn between lean production and the advantages to be gained as Japan's car makers began to undertake transnational production on a large scale. But in the opening years of the 1990s, just after Womack *et al.*'s appearance, two important occurrences in Japan can be marked, each of similar interest. First, a long period of growth in the Japanese national economy ended sharply: Japan, for decades a motor for the world economy, and for many observers a model to emulate, experienced a series of economic down-turns and an extended economic malaise. Second, Toyota saw its Japanese sales and production fall well below peak levels, again after a period of year on year growth in each which had mirrored the Japanese boom years of the 1980s.

Japan's industrial downturn

The so-called 'bubble period' in the recent history of Japan's national economy – of high year on year growth rates combined with a sustained inflation in asset prices, developing throughout and especially towards the end of the 1980s – was followed by a sharp drop in growth rates for both real and nominal GDP (in 1991–92), several years of bumping along, a brief recovery, a very deep recession (from 1997–1998), another brief recovery (in 2000), an exceedingly sharp collapse (in 2001), and gradually recovering growth since. The mark of these travails on Japan's reputation abroad has been severe.[10]

But manifestly, the same loss of reputation has not afflicted Japan's leading car maker, notwithstanding ostensibly similar downturn in industrial output in Japan. As with the wider national economy, the late 1980s saw 'abnormally high growth' in the domestic market for cars, with an 'explosion' – Kawahara's term – from 1987 up until 1990, at which point sales in Japan hit a peak level of over 7.7 million units, before a small decline in 1991 and then a steep fall over consecutive years. In the same year, domestic car production also hit a peak, albeit at the far higher level of around 13.5 million units, reflecting the enormous trade surpluses in cars enjoyed by Japan – the ensuing fall in output was even sharper than that for sales (see Kawahara, 1998: 237). Toyota, a principal subject in the story of lean production, experienced similar movements: escalating domestic sales and to a slightly less exaggerated extent escalating domestic production, followed by pronounced reductions in each as the bubble burst (*ibid.*). The reputation of Toyota abroad, however, was by not impacted by these movements. More recently, the Japanese firm – like the Japanese auto sector as a whole – is experiencing hard times at home, in a period of still weak growth and inflated fuel prices: but again one would predict that this will do little to dent Toyota's global reputation as a firm.

The reason for this is perhaps not difficult to state: Toyota is today – at least from a Westerner's perspective – viewed not only from the vantage point of its sales performance and production activities in Japan, but also as it appears on the world stage as a major transnational producer: it has (metaphorically) 'outgrown' Japan. There is perhaps an irony here, since many commentators both in the West and in Japan have seen in the globalising activities of Japanese firms (like Toyota) one possible source of the abiding depth of Japan's long recession of the 1990s.[11] Nor, for that matter, have any of Japan's car makers objected to the continuing protections afforded their home markets in Japan from import penetration (Schaede, 2007: 85). But irony aside, the reputation of Toyota is currently secured from the reputation of Japan.

Lean production and globalisation

There are several good reasons for highlighting this point. First is that the disassociation evident in the reputation of Toyota from that of Japan's home economy parallels in an appealing way the disassociation also evident between the public birth of lean production as a 'management panacea' – Lyddon's (1996: 77) phrase – in the pages of Womack *et al.* and the body of evidence adduced within for illustration and support. The globalisation of Toyota reflects a global appropriation of the production concept, the separation of fortunes for one a possible parable for other types of separation. Second, one can only wonder if the processes of globalisation that afflicted Japan's domestic economy in the 1990s also served to obscure the extent of mounting problems at Toyota in the late boom years of the 1980s, masking worker dissatisfaction – beyond the problems of recruitment and retention already acknowledged by the Japanese firm.

But finally it may be that the phenomenon of lean production, considered as an active force which can not only mould or shape judgement but give form to it, is best considered if developments in the international arena are kept to the fore of discussion. An inter-esting example to note is the thesis contained in Porter *et al.* (2000), to the effect that it is precisely because Japanese transnationals carried lean production to the West that the Japanese economy has now lost its international competitive advantage – an unlikely hypothesis from the viewpoint in this chapter, but also one that only makes sense in a particular international context, namely the changed fortunes of Japan.

In this regard, the two industrial crises, first in the West, and then in Japan, is a suggestive point from which to begin to develop a twinned perspective. If the detailed effects of a myth about pro-duction are felt principally in the workplace, it may also exist as a force at other levels – intruding, for example, into debates about the international economy and the benefits of free capital flows. A combined understanding is needed: at plant level, in international debate. A critique of lean production informs both.

Conclusions

In this chapter we take issue with received accounts of the IMVP world car assembly plant productivity survey, which gave birth to the words lean production. A detailed assessment of the data (necessary in any case given its abiding appeal) is worth pursuing seriously, because a more plausible reading of the evidence even when taken at its face value pushes one in a quite different direction to that actually taken. A deeper assessment also allows one to ask – contra the normal form of 'lean is mean' debate – whether what was uncovered was evidence of the limits of a specifically Japanese

variety of mature industrial capitalism, one combining high investment in labour-displacing equipment in factory processes with the
preservation of an extreme working day. From the viewpoint of illu-
minating the 'dark underside' of the Japanese economic miracle,
and putting a different perspective on the differences between the
evolution of auto industry practices in Japan *vis-à-vis* the West, this
takes us in an under-explored direction. This by no means denies
the continuing relevance of careful plant-level studies of the effects
of the introduction of production practices which have been associated with Japan, but we can – and do – reject the received inter-
pretation of what the IMVP study found.

Notes

1 A summary table of Japanese car assemblers' transplants in North
 America and Europe at the time of the IMVP world survey (for 1988) is
 provided in Womack *et al.* (1990: 202–3). Tomlinson (2005) provides a
 more global summary, up to 2000.
2 The quoted passage from Gilpin also draws attention to product quality
 as well as to lean production techniques (which no doubt many lean
 thinkers would describe as inseparable). In this chapter we focus on
 resource productivity: but for an interesting and alternative account of
 the complex data on product quality issues in the car market at around
 the time of the IMVP survey, of direct relevance to its stance on this
 issue, see Eberts and Eberts (1995: ch. 7). (A book suffused with an assertion of American strengths *vis-à-vis* Japanese product quality: but the
 treatment of the technical issues on quality measurement is careful, the
 discussion expansive.) For a corrective on the transformation of industry
 via the transplantation of lean production through the medium of FDI,
 see (for the British case) the example in Coffey (2006: 132–3).
3 Note that each of these regional averages was a weighted average (pre-
 sumably by plant output) and so would also reflect the size distribution
 of plants. The sites in question were all for volume producers, 'luxury'
 brands being treated separately in the survey.
4 The natural next step would be to break down the differences between
 average labour productivity in the European region from average productivity in the rest of the world into three separate components:
 (i) differences in average factory process automation; (ii) differences in
 estimated coefficients for the effects of automation on labour productivity; (iii) differences in intercepts. As Coffey (2006: 95–6) notes, the
 first difference looks small (referring to Figure 1, the average levels of
 automation between Europe and elsewhere were sufficiently close for a
 rough approximation to treat them as if converging at a shared point,
 a*). Data similar to that reported in Womack *et al.* (1990: see *ibid.*: 94–5)

suggests that somewhere in the region of one third again as much labour input was used in Europe for an average completed task set as was required (on average) for plants elsewhere in the world – give or take: this difference, in turn, split fairly evenly between differences in estimated coefficients and intercepts.

Explanations for the relevant indices are set out in Krafcik (1988) (for labour) and Krafcik (1989) (for automation), and fully reviewed in Coffey (2006: Chapter 3). Topics covered include treatments of vertical structure, product size and variety. As Coffey (*ibid.*) shows, the automation index implies a labour-displacing technology, relevant for discussion in the next section.

5   In the table of regional (weighted) labour productivity averages Womack *et al.* (1990: 85) state that there were a total of 22 sites based in Europe for volume producers, of which 13 were indigenous and 9 were split between US and Japanese firm owned plants. However, only 18 points are displayed on the scatter of observations on labour productivity and automation for Europe (see *ibid.*: 94–5). Assuming that the larger reported total subsumes the smaller, between five and nine of the 'poorly' performing Europe-based sites were in fact transplants owned and managed by either American or Japanese transnationals.

6   The tabled data for regional (weighted) averages on labour productivity shows absolutely no evidence that the combined 'performance' of American and Japanese firms in Europe was 'better' than the indigenous performance, using the IMVP labour productivity index: 35.3 hours for each completed task cycle for transplants to Europe, 35.5 hours for indigenous firms.

7   By contrast, in Britain which has relatively long working hours compared to other countries in the EC (but not pushed to the extremes indicated in the above report), this has coincided with perennial angst about underinvestment in plant and equipment.

8   Although we should be prepared for complex findings. Coffey and Thornley (2009), for example, present the findings of a (British) Ford factory case study in which a 'strong' union branch attempted to embed hard won rights in the management handbook by framing these rights in juxtaposition with the words 'lean production': one must not overlook workers' self-activity. In this instance, the plant was shortly closed thereafter – a possible consequence.

9   The estimates are drawn from Coffey and Thornley (2006b). Readers interested in a fuller discussion are referred to Coffey (2006: Chapter 5), which explains in detail, and provides a contextual discussion that includes some notes on historical antecedents in the West. Some general discussions of the Toyota experiments, reflecting the immediate impact on the literature, are included in a number of the contributions published in Sandberg (1995). Note that the logic of line segmentation does imply some intensification of work-rate for employees: stoppages affecting the entire assembly line would be avoided, while workers on segments afflicted by stoppages would have to fix the problem and then

step up a gear to restore buffers. Research is needed on (a) how this is received by workers and (b) other changes in the system.

10 See Werner (2007) for relevant series on the long Japanese recession; Coates (2007) for a good review of the changing status of Japan as an international economic role model.

11 Western proponents of this view include Cowling and Tomlinson (2000; 2003) who argue that by forging 'national champions' to compete on the international plane the Japanese state left itself open to lobbying activities by the same large firms to allow them to source production overseas through outward foreign direct investment (FDI). The accompanying re-direction of investment is held in this view to have seriously undermined Japan's domestic economy. There is now a lively debate about kūdōka – the 'hollowing out' of Japan's industrial base' (see, for example, Bailey and Sugden, 2007; and references within) – although as Schaede (2007: 82–3) observes, fears within Japan itself on this head date as far back as the 1970s. Of particular concern has been the evident collapse of small firm structures (see all of the above). Note that while broadly compelling, a necessary complement to this type of political economy requires some acknowledgement of the pressures placed on Japan in the 1980s to 'open' up to Western firms and to accede to policy realignments to end the huge trade surpluses it had built up at the expense of competitors abroad (see Coates, 2000; 2007).

References

Bailey, D. and Sugden, R. (2007) 'Kudoka, restructuring and possibilities for industrial policy in Japan' in Bailey, D., Coffey, D. and Tomlinson, P.R. (eds) *Crisis or Recovery in Japan: State and Industrial Economy*. Cheltenham and Northampton, MA: Edward Elgar.

Benders, J. and Morita, M. (2004) 'Changes in Toyota Motors' operations management', *International Journal of Production Research*, vol. 42, no. 3, pp. 433–4.

Coates, D. (2000) *Models of Capitalism: Growth and Stagnation in the Modern Era*. Oxford and Malden, Massachusetts: Polity Press.

Coates, D. (2007) 'The rise and fall of Japan as a model of "progressive capitalism"', in Bailey, D., Coffey, D. and Tomlinson, P.R. (eds) *Crisis or Recovery in Japan: State and Industrial Economy*. Cheltenham and Northampton, MA: Edward Elgar, pp. 179–96.

Coffey, D. (2006) *The Myth of Japanese Efficiency: The World Car Industry in a Globalizing Age*. Cheltenham and Northampton, MA: Edward Elgar.

Coffey, D. and Thornley, C. (2006a) 'Automotive Assembly: Automation, Motivation and Lean Production Reconsidered', *Assembly Automation: The International Journal of Assembly Technology and Management*, vol. 26, no. 2, pp. 98–103.

Coffey, D. and Thornley, C. (2006b) 'Changes in Toyota Motors' operations management further considered: line-stoppage frequencies and theoretical cost efficiencies', mimeo.

Coffey, D. and Thornley, C. (2009) *Globalization and the Varieties of Capitalism Debate: New Labour, Economic Policy and the Abject State*. Palgrave Macmillan (forthcoming).

Cowling, K. and Tomlinson, P.R. (2000) 'The Japanese Crisis – A Case of Strategic Failure?', *The Economic Journal*, 110(464): F358–F381.

Cowling, K. and Tomlinson, P.R. (2003) 'Industrial policy, transnational corporations and the problem of "hollowing out" in Japan', in D. Coffey and C. Thornley (eds) *Industrial and Labour Market Policy and Performance: Issues and Perspectives*. London and New York: Routledge, pp. 62–82.

Eberts, R. and Eberts, A. (1995) *The Myths of Japanese Quality*. Upper Saddle River, New Jersey: Prentice Hall Publishers.

Gilpin, R. (2000) *The Challenge of Global Capitalism: The World Economy in the 21st Century*. Princeton and Oxford: Princeton University Press.

Kawahara, A. (1998) *The Origin of Competitive Strength: Fifty Years of the Auto Industry in Japan and the U.S.* Springer: Verlag-Tokyo.

Kenney, M. and Florida, R. (1993) *Beyond Mass Production: The Japanese System and Its Transfer to the US*. Oxford and New York: Oxford University Press.

Krafcik, J.F. (1988) *A Methodology for Assembly Plant Performance Determination*, IMVP Research Affiliates. Cambridge, MA: MIT, October 1988.

Krafcik, J.F. (1989) *A Comparative Analysis of Assembly Plant Automation*, IMVP International Policy Forum. Cambridge, MA: MIT, May 1989.

Lyddon, D. (1996) 'The Myth of Mass Production and the Mass Production of Myth', *Historical Studies in Industrial Relations*, March.

Monden, Y. (1998) *Toyota Production System: An Integrated Approach to Just-in-Time* (3rd edn). Norcross, Georgia: Engineering and Management Press.

Moody, K. (1997) *Workers in a Lean World: Unions in the International Economy*. Verso: London and New York.

Porter, M.E., Takeuchi, H. and Sakakibara, M. (2000) *Can Japan Compete?*. Hampshire and London: MacMillan Press Ltd.

Sandberg, A. (1995) *Enriching Production: Perspectives on Volvo's Uddevalla plant as an alternative to lean production*. Aldershort, England and Brookfield, Vermont: Avebury.

Schaede, U. (2007) 'Globalization and the Japanese subcontractor system' in Bailey, D., Coffey, D. and Tomlinson, P.R. (eds) *Crisis of Recovery in Japan: State and Industrial Economy*, Cheltenham and Northampton, MA: Edward Elgar.

Tomlinson, P.R. (2005) 'The overseas entry patterns of Japanese automobile assemblers 1960–2000: globalization of manufacturing capacity and the role of strategic contingency', *International Journal of Automotive Technology and Management*, vol. 5, no. 3, pp. 284–304.

Werner, R.A. (2007) 'The cause of Japan's recession and the lessons for the world', in Bailey, D., Coffey, D. and Tomlinson, P.R. (eds) *Crisis or Recovery in Japan: State and Industrial Economy*. Cheltenham and Northampton, MA: Edward Elgar.

Williams, K., Haslam, C., Williams, J., Cutler, T., Adcroft, A. and Johal, S. (1994) *Cars: Analysis, History, Cases*. Oxford: Berghahn.

Womack, J., Jones, D.T. and Roos, D. (1990) *The Machine That Changed the World*. New York: Harper Collins.

Womack, J. and Jones, D.T. (2003) *Lean Thinking: Banish Waste and Create Wealth in Your Corporation* (2nd Edition). Bath: Simon and Schuster.

Part II

Developments in the International Car Industry: The National-based Perspective

4
Scope for Policymaking in a Globalised Economy: The Case of Car Assembly in Belgium

Geert Van Hootegem and Rik Huys

An industry under threat

The spatial organisation of the automobile production in Europe has been changing quite rapidly over the last decade. This change has been strongly affected by the enlargement of the European Union towards Central and Eastern Europe (Layan and Lung, 1995). The search by the car industry for new peripheries in new member states thereby threatens the former peripheries. Belgium is particularly concerned by this reorganisation as the country cannot be considered to be in the core of Europe's car industry. It does not house important decision-making powers in the industry, nor does it hold important design, R&D or production activities that invoke a higher-order and diversified type of know-how. As the industry is dominated by the four 'screwdriver plants' for cars that are highly dependent on foreign headquarters,[1] Lung attributes Belgium with a peripheral status in the automobile industry (Lung, 2002). The fact that Belgium recently lost its longstanding status as largest car assembler per capita in the world to Slovakia is testimony to this redistribution of the division of labour within the European car industry.

In view of these threats it is not surprising that most Belgian car assembly plants have had their fair share of restructuring and reduction of manpower.[2] Each time such a crisis erupts, politicians at the local, regional and national level flock to the assembly plant to express their support and feverishly consult with management and employees on how to limit further job losses. But each time the question also arises as to what, if anything, policy-makers can do when confronted with the decisions of such global players as the automobile groups.

The impact of local factors determining location decisions of multinational companies is not obvious. All countries, regions and even cities parade with their political, juridical and economic framework. Companies set them against each other as a result of which this framework continues to lose its impact on decision-making. Due to globalisation, the power of national and regional governments to direct and influence their economies has shrunk considerably. National or regional economies no longer function as autonomous systems of wealth creation since national borders are no longer significant in the conduct and organisation of economic activity. This is especially true for Belgium as it is Europe's most open economy.[3] And it is especially true for the car industry that is dominated by a decreasing number of multinationals that integrate national and regional economies into global production networks. Rather than nation states, it is global corporate capital that exercises the decisive influence over the organisation, location and distribution of economic power and resources in this industry.

Despite these objections, policy-makers are still very much pushed to get involved. First and foremost the car assembly industry remains an important pillar of the Belgian economy. A peculiar aspect of the industry is the high concentration of employment at one single location. The four car assembly plants in Belgium are not the biggest employers in the country, but they have the largest number of employees under one single roof. This implies that decisions on investment or disinvestment have a huge impact on the local labour market. As the consequences of a massive lay-off inevitably will turn up on their plate, governments may as well try to influence decisions beforehand instead of being left to pick up the pieces. Additionally, the car assembly industry employs a huge number of unqualified people, which constitutes a risk group in the labour market. A more proportionate participation of risk groups in the labour process is a prime concern of labour market policy. It is therefore understandable that the sectors in which they work receive particular attention.

These considerations pushed the Flemish government[4] to take the initiative for a more preventive and structured approach for the car assembly industry. A task force for the car assembly industry was set up in 2004 as a tripartite committee, involving all the top managers in the sector, several trade union leaders, senior civil servants and key cabinet staff members of the Flemish government. Its mission was to outline an optimal policy for the sector and to issue a final report proposing concrete policy measures aimed at keeping vehicle assembly plants in the region. The task force regularly met to monitor progress on agreed action points.

This task force is a prime test case to assess the extent to which governments are able to respond to the pressure exercised by the global economy. In the following paragraphs three important competitive factors which influence the decisions of production allocation of models, production volume and investments to individual assembly plants are discussed. These are related to working time arrangements, the establishment of an extensive and efficient supplier network and the availability of a qualified workforce. Then, the decisions taken by the task force in the auto sector in Belgium in order to increase the level of competitiveness of the national auto sector are presented and evaluated in relation with the competitive factors. If these measures made any difference to the assembly plants, it may prove to be of continuing relevance to national and regional governments in shaping their economy.

Be creative with time

In the last decades a lot of tinkering has occurred on working and operating times in the Belgian car assembly plants. These changes were aimed at an extension of operating times by means of additional shifts as well as at an increased flexibility with which the available production capacity can be applied.

Extension of operating hours: During the 60s a job in the car assembly industry was essentially a nine to five job. As research on the well-being of employees in car assembly plants at that time reported 'what employees find most favourable is the fact that there is no shift system so that a normal family life is possible' (Coetsier, 1966). However, during the 70s and 80s most plants introduced a two-shift system, while in the 90s a three-shift system became common. The Volkswagen plant in Brussels ultimately introduced a fourth shift during weekends, by which a new record was set in the number of operating hours for an assembly plant. In a European, and even a worldwide, perspective, the Belgian car assembly plants exploited the path of extension in operating times quickly. While early in the 90s a three-shift production was still uncommon in the car assembly industry (Lehndorff, 1991), this was already common place in most Belgian plants.

Flexibility of working times: A great diversity has been introduced in the working time in the Belgian car assembly plants. The past decade witnessed almost all imaginable schedules: shifts of eight, nine or ten hours; working weeks of three, three and two-thirds, four or five days, sometimes including regular Saturday work; varying working times during the week or a varying number of working days during the week. This diversity is the result of plant specific sophistication in order to maximise capacity and flexibility within the existing technical restrictions. While a number of legal restrictions exist, if social partners agree, deviations are possible. As Lehndorff concluded in his inventory of working times in the European car industry: 'in Belgium almost anything is possible, as long as social partners unite' (Lehndorff, 1991: 45). This is also the result of industrial relations in the Belgian car industry, in which the weight lies at the company level. The company agreements between management and local union leaders allow for solutions tailored to the needs of individual plants.

In addition, car assembly plants in Belgium make use of the system of 'temporary unemployment' by which blue collar workers can be temporarily put on unemployment benefit for economic or technical reasons with little cost to the company. This provides the plants with a cheaper manoeuvrability downwards to reduce manpower compared to other countries where the necessary flexibility is more likely to be achieved upwards by means of overtime. This creativity in dealing with working and operating times has undoubtedly contributed to the attractiveness of Belgian car assembly plants. As the capital intensity in car assembly increases, it becomes more important for plants to operate the installed expensive production capacity on a continuous basis. And in view of the saturation and the fluctuations on the car market, the flexibility with which the plant can address the swings in demand is an additional asset.

But as is the case with all competitive strengths, an advantage lasts only as long as competitors do not dispose of the same strong points. While Belgian plants have been precursors in the extension of operating times, in the mean time many European car assembly plants have followed this path. The comparative advantage that came from an extension of operating times has thereby disappeared. Even worse, it has turned into a disadvantage. Taxes and social security contributions on bonuses for shift and night work are higher in Belgium than in most other European countries.

This higher labour cost for continuous production is not without risks, since the extension of operating times in car assembly plants is a major cause of overcapacity, which in its turn leads to plant closures. As more plants assemble cars round the clock, production capacity continues to increase and overcapacity grows. But the market for cars – at least in Western Europe – is fairly static. In other words, car assembly plants are involved in a 'zero-sum game' (Lehndorff, 1999). The increased capacity in one plant is then an additional reason to close other car assembly plants. Plants operating below the new norm of three-shift production are especially vulnerable.

While over a decade ago, the implementation of a night shift by Belgian car assembly plants was a means to achieve a competitive advantage, once installed they turned out to be too expensive. Pressures were then exerted on the government to remove the competitive disadvantage by reducing taxation and social security contributions on shift and night work.

A similar story holds for the flexibility to deploy employees. In this respect Belgium maintains a unique position in Europe through its system of temporary unemployment. But in neighbouring countries the annualisation of working time in which employees can be called upon to work more in certain periods while compensating these additional hours over the year or over several years has flourished. As a result, the flexibility of Belgian car assembly plants no longer stands out. Again, pressures are exerted to enlarge the possibilities to deploy employees flexibly in the car industry.

Past experiences on the issue of working and operating times therefore seem to validate the incapacity of governments to direct and influence company decisions in a global economy. While some measures may result in a competitive advantage for local plants, these are mainly short term as governments and unions in different countries are set against each other in order to engage in further concession bargaining. As a result an increase in unusual and flexible working hours throughout the industry seems inevitable.

Are there measures which can stop this downward spiral and convert the issue of working time in a 'win–win' situation for employees and companies? It is clear that a further increase in flexibility is on the wish list of management in car assembly plants, but how can this be reconciled with the wishes of employees and their representatives to improve working conditions? In this respect, it is striking that in the recent ESWT-survey[5] of the European Foundation, employee representatives mentioned the introduction or extension of flexi-time or working-time accounts as the most desirable measure for employees to achieve a better work–life balance (Riedmann, 2006). Considering the demands of management in car assembly plants, it must be possible to combine their flexibility requirements with the desires for individual flexibility and employee security. The challenge therefore is to link the different wishes from individual employees regarding their working hours to the requirements in 'collective' fluctuations from the company.

Plants themselves can make an obvious contribution to improve this combination by providing employees – e.g. within the framework of teamwork – more autonomy regarding their leave arrangements. From a policy perspective, forms of individual flexibility that already exist in Belgium such as 'time credit'[6] can be applied as an instrument to combine flexibility requirements of organisations with greater employee security. The use of time credit, not merely based on the individual wishes of employees, but as a means to bridge business fluctuations in companies, could contribute to the reduction of lay-offs.[7] In general terms, such measures require a shift of the financial support by government from, for example, providing a bonus for taking early retirement. The alternative might be to retain workers for their experience through downturns in the business cycle (e.g. bonus for taking on time credit).

While 'flexicurity' is a concept that recently enjoyed considerable popularity in European countries,[8] the longstanding Belgian system of temporary unemployment is a prime example of flexicurity. It is a policy measure that combines the flexibility requirements of companies with contractual security for employees. This system must therefore be staunchly defended against objections from the European Commission concerning unfair competition. Furthermore, the flexicurity of employees with temporary contracts can be improved by means of collective pooling. The Belgian car assembly plants are located close to one another allowing for an exchange of employees. While car assembly plants may undergo the same seasonal fluctuations, this does not hold for the considerable fluctuations linked to the model cycle. The recruitment needs of the car assembly plants are therefore spread out. Pooling is also an option in supplier companies. Especially when some suppliers may not be able to extend their contract with the car assembly plant, employees can be employed by other or new suppliers. These measures would prevent employees being lost to the sector due to short-term fluctuations in demand. Moreover, they would provide employees with better security in an environment that requires more flexibility. As such these are examples of longer-term policy measures governments can take to support the competitive position of local car assembly plants and at the same time avoid deteriorating working conditions for employees.

Anchoring of car assembly plants through development of a supplier industry

While Belgium has always been a very open economy with important economic sectors dominated by foreign companies, concern has been growing on the loss of influence of Belgian actors in the economy. Since the 80s a growing number of companies in traditionally Belgian-owned sectors such as food or banking and insurance were taken over by foreign companies. This was not, which is not matched by foreign investments of Belgian companies. In addition the relative autonomy of local management in traditionally foreign-owned sectors such as the car assembly industry has been reduced as multinationals shift power to centrally governed product divisions (Daems, 1990). Thus, plant managers in Belgium get more of a role as ambassadors representing the interests of foreign companies to Belgian government, rather than being involved in the strategic decisions in the Belgian plants.

The debate in Belgium on supportive policy measures towards plants of multinational companies is therefore strongly influenced by an 'anchoring' perspective. The idea is to embed the activities of the plant in such a way that a sudden delocalisation becomes unlikely. As Belgium has few home-grown multinational companies itself and depends to a large extent on subsidiaries of foreign multi-nationals, this may be an understandable perspective. But it remains at odds with the strategies of the car groups themselves since their aim is for a maximum mobility through a reduction of fixed costs.

The reduction of fixed costs and their conversion into variable costs that vary in proportion to the number of cars assembled acquires an ever increasing priority for car groups. On the one hand the costs to keep up with – and if possible take the lead in – the increasing pace of technological evolution in the development and production of cars are huge. On the other hand, the saturated car market in Europe has acquired a cyclical nature, in which the reduction of fixed costs and their shift into variable costs are an important means to survive the downturns in the business cycle.

In order to lower fixed costs and make them variable, car groups apply a number of strategies. Joint-ventures and mergers between car groups help to spread investment costs. The extension of operating hours of plants yields a faster result from investments. The platform strategy of car groups, in which a maximum number of models is assembled on the same platform, allows for the spread of R&D costs over a greater number of cars. This platform strategy also provides car groups with a greater flexibility in the allocation of models between their assembly plants producing different models on the same platform. As such investments become less model specific, this decreases their 'anchoring' in a given location.

Outsourcing of activities is yet another strategy that fits this approach. Outsourcing by car assembly plants is not merely confined to supporting activities, but includes also the assembly of components and even whole modules which were previously done by car assembly plants themselves. Such outsourcing lowers the initial investment in production capacity for the car group and makes these assembly costs variable. But the achievement of this aim implies a higher mobility for car groups and thereby again less 'anchoring' of extant production capacity.

In addition there is a clear trend towards a reduction in the number of players in the supplier business. Through higher requirements of car groups, existing local suppliers risk being pushed aside by global players 'following' the car groups. These global suppliers are even more mobile than the car groups themselves and their contribution to the anchoring of the latter is highly questionable.

Therefore the idea of policy-makers to anchor car assembly plants through supporting the development of supplier networks around them seems essentially flawed. It seems that government attempts to accommodate the demands of the car companies may deliver a short-term competitive advantage for local plants but is unable to exercise a decisive influence over location decisions. Even worse, the efforts of governments to support the development of suppliers parks, makes the industry more mobile thereby facilitating possible future delocalisation decisions. Once more, the question arises as to whether policy measures are possible that support the development of the supplier industry and at the same time boost the longer-term position of the car industry. Indeed the supplier industry in Belgium remained relatively underdeveloped, despite an enormous number of cars being assembled in the country itself and in neighbouring regions.

Currently, many companies on supplier parks in the immediate vicinity of car assembly plants are very vulnerable as they have only one customer. When the car assembly plant closes down, they have few chances of survival. Governments can appoint 'supplier consultants' who assist suppliers to find new clients and applications for their products, reducing their dependency on car assembly plants and opening up a new growth potential for economic activity. Such diversification efforts as undertaken on the industrial supplier park near Ford-Genk have proven to be possible. In the process, new employment opportunities were created and not merely a shift of employment from car assembly plants to suppliers. A more active role can be played by governments taking on the investment of the facilities on the supplier parks since the initial investment cost in this infrastructure is an obstacle for suppliers seeking to establish a plant locally.

This fits the idea of supporting a central supplier park for the four car assembly plants in Belgium that are all located within a stone's throw of one another. Apart from the collective provision of infrastructure and supportive services, economies of scale could be achieved in this way. In addition demand fluctuations of individual car assembly plants would have a less dramatic impact on the activities – and employees – of supplier plants. Governments could appoint intermediaries establishing contact between car assembly plants to overcome the initial resistance between competitors so as to realise the centralised supply of a number of – non-critical – components.

But most importantly, the nature of activities in the supplier industry needs to be developed. The car industry in Belgium is characterised by activities with a relatively low added value. For decades Belgium boasted about being the worlds' biggest car assembler per inhabitant, but regarding design, research and development or the production of important components such as engines or transmissions, Belgium is not a 'car country'. In order to achieve an anchoring of supplier activities, these activities should not be restricted to logistics and assembly, but need to include activities with higher added value that compensate for the high wage cost.

Several government programmes have already proven to be fruitful in this respect. Noteworthy is 'Flander's Drive' for which the Flemish government provided an important subsidy. It concerns the investment in and the operation of a high-tech test infrastructure and a computing and design centre that assists Flemish companies in the mechanical development of components and substructures for vehicles. A second part of the project involves sensitisation, networking, technological advice and common research. Both initiatives support innovation in the supplier sector that can rely on a technical staff and a performance infrastructure.

The effective deployment of qualified employees

Education and training is another major area in which public institutions can play an active role in supporting the successful operation of companies. Indeed, vocational training is one of the few areas where direct support to the car industry is still allowed by the European Commission. Developments in product, the production process and work organisation require changing qualifications from employees. By means of continuous learning opportunities employees can renew their qualifications, allowing their companies to adapt to new circumstances.

There has been considerable mobilisation around the issue of lifelong learning in Belgium, in response to European targets on participation in education and training. Yet in general, participation in Belgium lags behind European averages. Time is often lacking in organisations to enhance participation in training. At the same time when such time is available, e.g. during down-turns, car assembly plants frequently make blue collar workers temporarily unemployed. The specific arrangement in Belgium on temporary unemployment thereby contributes, especially in times of economic downturn, pushing back lifelong learning compared with other countries, where downturns are more used as an opportunity for training.

It would however be a mistake to restrict learning in organisations to receiving formal training. Learning in and during the execution of the job itself is for many employees potentially a much more effective means to renew and expand their qualifications than the participation in formal training. But this requires that the job is designed in such a way that it offers learning opportunities (Huys and Van Hootegem, 2004). If the job on the assembly line remains limited to the acquisition of speed in the execution of standardised tasks, there are few opportunities for employees to learn from and during work. If on the other hand new forms of work organisation lead to the allocation of responsibilities to assembly line employees on quality control, maintenance, problem-solving, communication, they can acquire diversified qualifications which are useful when adapting to changing circumstances.

The extent to which jobs offer learning opportunities to employees, is therefore dependent on the kind of work organisation implemented in the company. This work organisation is one of the few factors in which car assembly plants themselves have some leverage. In general, the manoeuvring space of Belgian car assembly plants is very limited as the cars they assemble are neither designed nor sold by them. They are at the mercy of the assignments allocated by headquarters. Car assembly plants can 'merely' assemble the type and volume of cars allocated to them in the most efficient and flexible way and according to the quality imperative.

The work organisation applied in the assembly process is a major factor where plants can make the difference *vis-à-vis* other assembly plants in the car group. In the car industry, the work organisation of Japanese plants created a furore in past decades. On this basis a model of lean production has been advanced as most effective. Even though objections may be raised against this model, it points to work organisation as one of the most critical factors in the performance of plants. Lean production does not attribute performance differences between plants to the level of automation, culture or wage costs, but primarily to the implementation of a lean work organisation (Womack *et al.*, 1990).

As work organisation is considered to be so important in the performance of car assembly plants, it is striking that this issue receives little attention in the supporting policy initiatives of governments. There is a realisation that innovation in a broad sense is important for companies, but innovation policy is dominated by technological innovation, even though innovations in work organisation have often proved to be the decisive factor overall.

To support new forms of work organisation, innovation funds provided by government agencies must urgently include non-technological innovation. In this way the knowledge and diffusion of successful work organisations can be enhanced. Research into the work organisation of Belgian assembly plants (Huys, 2001) shows that there is no such thing as a 'Belgian approach' in work organisation. Most plants are merely going by the compass of their headquarters which essentially offer a version of lean production.

Yet the Volvo-Ghent plant has enjoyed more autonomy on this issue within the former Volvo group. Over the past decades the plant acquired more extensive experience with new forms of work organisation (Huys and Van Hootegem, 1999) that can be useful to transfer to other plants as well as their suppliers. The establishment of an infrastructure for the transfer of such knowledge and experience on issues regarding work organisation could contribute to the competitiveness of the plants.

Presentation and evaluation of task force decisions

In June 2005 the task force on the car assembly industry published its report outlining an action plan for the sector. The action points concern labour costs, flexibility, innovation, administrative support, training, logistics and cost-savings in energy. An overview is provided in Table 4.1. Since the report's publication several of the proposed policy measures have been adopted.

Support of national or regional governments for the car industry is restricted by European framework legislation. Most of actions taken are therefore 'horizontal' measures that are in principle applicable for all companies. However, as some of the measures are related to issues which are widely applied in the car industry, some

Table 4.1   Support measures agreed in the task force car industry

Action point	Commentary
1: Reduction of wage costs	In 2005 a reduction in social security contributions on shift work of 5.63% was enacted. In 2007 this should be increased to 10.7%. A reduction of 1% on shift work corresponds to a reduction in total labour costs of 0.4%.
2: Permanent monitoring of wage costs	A methodology is elaborated to monitor wage costs in the car assembly industry in relation to neighbouring countries.
3: Introduction of time	Agreement between sector and social saving partners in 2006 to enable time saving and a plus – minus account. For companies this allows for adaptation to production fluctuations through a variable working week. For employees this allows for differentiation in working time during their career according to their needs through time saving.
4: Vehicle and industry of the future	Research on successful innovation strategies for the car industry in order to survive after 2015.
5: Proactive sensibilisation on process innovation	The Flemish Institute for the Promotion of Innovation through Science and Technology will sensitise and guide car plants to aid in the implementation of proposals for funding innovative projects.
6: Broadening of the innovation concept	Funds for technological innovation are broadened to include support for process innovations which are non-technological. There is also an additional support of 10% for R&D projects.
7: Innovative outsourcing by governments	The government introduces a purchasing policy that requires technological solutions. It takes the car industry as its pilot project.
8: Account managers for the industry	Account managers are appointed to accompany each car assembly plant in its contacts with governments.
9: Better rapport between demand and labour market supply	Measures to increase attractiveness of technical courses in school education. Each car assembly plant is appointed an account manager from the employment office which offers guidance in recruitment and training. For professions with a lack of available candidates, the employment office makes an action plan and the procedure to receive work permits for employees from new member states is simplified.

Table 4.1   Support measures agreed in the task force car industry –
continued

Action point	Commentary
10: Cooperation in logistics	A study is made on possibilities of multimodal transport. Longer trucks are allowed on certain routes and under certain conditions. The accessibility of the infrastructure on supplier parks is improved.
11: Cheaper energy through a review of green power policy	Juridical and practical obstacles to generate green power are eliminated.
12: Lowering of taxes on energy products	Exemption or lowering of taxes on energy products for companies that conclude an environmental covenant.

of the horizontal measures are to the particular benefit of the four car assembly plants.

The three competitive factors discussed above – working time regulations, supplier industry, formal and informal learning – are reflected in the action points identified by the task force. We refer respectively to the actions combining employees' wishes on flexibility with those of companies (action point 3), to improve infrastructure on supplier parks (action point 10), to broaden the innovation concept to include aspects of work organisation for application for innovation funds (action point 6) and to improve companies' training policies (action point 9). Above we have shown that it is possible for governments to take measures supporting the competitive position of local car assembly plants while avoiding mere concession bargaining. These are good examples of longer-term policy measures governments can take to support the development of activities in the car industry invoking a higher-order and more diversified type of know-how. It supports the idea of the sector moving to what Lung (2002) calls the core of Europe's car sector, making it less vulnerable to the search for new peripheries by the car industry.

Yet the emphasis in many of the other action points is on the reduction of costs for car assembly plants, such as energy costs (action points 11 and 12) and labour costs (action points 1 and 2). Particularly the reduction in gross labour costs is singled out as the most important outcome of the task force. There was a concern that the Belgian car industry could lose its wage-cost advantage over Germany, where many of the sister plants of Belgian car assembly plants are located. In Belgium, additional wage bonuses that workers receive for night time or shift working are currently liable for payment of social security contributions whereas, in countries like Germany, these wage bonuses are exempt from social security tax. To counteract this national disadvantage, the Belgian federal government has decided to lower social security contributions on shift work to 10 per cent by 2007.

It is however unlikely that the comparative advantage achieved in this way will be long-lasting. Any reduction of taxes in one country is followed by additional pressures of multinational companies on governments in other countries to 'restore' the comparative disadvantage, giving way to a downward spiral. This is exemplified by the agreement of Volkswagen with German labour unions to extend working hours from just under 29 hours to 33–35 hours per week without pay increase. After this agreement, the assembly of the Volkswagen-Golf was shifted from Brussels to the German car assembly plants of Volkswagen in Wolfsburg and Mosel with the loss of 3,500 jobs. The reduction of gross labour costs achieved by the task force is therefore already being offset by measures in other countries.

In addition, as taxes on shift and night work were originally aimed as a break on the application of unusual working hours, such a tax reduction is at odds with the aim of policy-makers to improve quality of working life as an important means to increase labour market participation of older employees and delay average retirement age, which are both strikingly low in Belgium. In order to increase the attractiveness to work until retirement age, the government together with all social partners solemnly signed a pact at the beginning of the century setting the goal to improve the quality of working life (Pact van Vilvoorde, 2001). Despite these intentions, the government at the same time facilitates shift and night work in the hope of achieving a competitive advantage for the car assembly plants over their foreign competitors. Yet studies have shown that shift and night work is detrimental to human health and thereby contributes to early retirement (Costa, 1996).

As a way out of this short-term cost reduction approach, we would advocate a more central place for the initiatives in action point 6 of the task force plan. This action point aims to broaden innovation funding from technological innovation to innovation on work organisation and thereby provides a possible alternative approach for support of the car assembly industry. In a 'high road' approach to competitiveness, the emphasis is put on quality and innovation by qualified employees in order to make the difference compared with low-wage countries. A more holistic approach to the shaping of work tasks and decentralisation of decision-making leads to the enhanced use of human skills and knowledge (Totterdill *et al.*, 2002).

The Auto 5000 production concept set up by Volkswagen in its Wolfsburg plant is an example of an attempt to put a 'high road' competitive strategy into practice in order to ensure a continued presence of car assembly in Germany (Schumann *et al.*, 2006). The fact that such a concerted effort by governments and social partners to aim for organisational innovation has not been addressed by the task force, may be attributed to the absence of headquarters or decision-making powers concerning the car assembly industry in Belgium. Arguably this means that there is not the necessary backing to put new concepts into practice.

Indeed most car assembly plants in Belgium follow the recipes proposed by the advocates of lean production (Womack *et al.*, 1990). Research on work organisation in the Belgian car assembly plants (Huys, 2001) illustrates the growing intensification of labour. This implies that plants scrap parallel assembly lines in favour of one single assembly line, scrap buffers between production stages in favour of a tightened assembly line and scrap pre-assemblies and off-line jobs in favour of work at the line. In consequence, an increasing number of assembly jobs have a shorter work cycle, increased line pacing and above all greater standardisation requiring little or no qualification and offering few learning opportunities.

However as the case of the Belgian Volvo-Ghent plant shows, the elaboration of new forms of work organisation in car assembly is also possible in the Belgian context. Although still very much based on line assembly, workers on the assembly line are also involved in off-line tasks. Work organisation at the plant delegates a set of indirect tasks to assembly line workers themselves resulting in a substantial transfer of tasks and responsibilities from line management and staff departments to the shop floor. The Volvo-plant in Ghent is also the only car assembly plant in Belgium that has continued to expand over the last decades, in terms of production volume as well as employment. It thereby points once more to the importance of work organisation for the performance of car assembly plants.

The action plan therefore fails in our view to focus efforts on the enhancement and exchange of knowledge of new forms of work organisation. If our car assembly plants apply the same lean production recipes on work organisation as is done in new member states with considerably lower wage costs, how can a competitive advantage be maintained? In copying a recipe on work organisation, car assembly plants are losing a trump card in one of the few areas where they can make a difference. As long as a work organisation that neither uses nor develops skills and qualifications is maintained, governments risk being sucked into a low road approach aimed at cost reductions in the hope of delaying delocalisation. If that is the outcome, the costs incurred would have been better directed to the development of more knowledge-intensive activities in the economy.

As such, the main points of the action plan are testimony to a defensive 'low road' approach in which the hope is that short-term cost-driven measures will keep activities here or at least slow their delocalisation. This supports the argument that due to globalisation governments must increasingly manage their national economies in such a way as to adapt them to the pressures of transnational market forces (Leys, 2001).

Notes

1 Volvo-Ghent, Opel-Antwerp, Ford-Genk and Volkswagen-Brussels.
2 Next to closure of Renault-Vilvoorde in 1997, Ford-Genk endured in 2003 the shift of Transit-production to Turkey and the cancellation of the promised investments for the assembly of the Ford-Focus. In 2006 Volkswagen-Brussels lost Golf assembly to German plants and had to become an Audi-plant with a reduced workforce. Finally in 2007 Opel announced that the successor of the Astra will not be assembled in Antwerp, leading to the dismissal of 1,400 employees.
3 Defined as the level of import and export related to its Gross National Product (Sociaal-Economisch Rapport voor Vlaanderen, Brussel: SERV, 2005).
4 As a federalised nation, a significant element of responsibility for economic and labour market policies are assigned to the regions. As three of

the four car assembly plants are located in the Flemish region, with Volkswagen-Brussels just at the border of Flanders with many workers from the Flemish region, the car assembly industry is mainly a concern for Flanders. For some measures (still the preserve of national responsibility) consultations were necessary with the national government, but the initiative to set up a structured policy on the car assembly industry originates from the Flemish government.

5 European establishment survey on working time and work-life balance by the European Foundation for the Improvement of Living and Working Conditions.

6 Since 2002, employees have a right to use a 'time credit' in which they can temporarily limit or interrupt work without terminating their work contract. In this period the employee is entitled to benefit under the terms of the framework of unemployment insurance. The aim of the time credit system is to offer a time relief for those in work while at the same time supporting labour market participation of older employees by allowing a more gradual exit from the labour market.

7 As an example, suppliers of Ford-Genk in 2003 fired approximately 3,000 employees as a consequence of the restructuring in the plant and the reduction of production volume. In 2006 more than 1,500 employees were again recruited, as a result of the success of their two new models. A financial bonus for employees in companies undertaking restructuring who wish to apply for a time credit could have prevented the initial layoffs and the loss of trained and experienced employees to the industry as a whole.

8 The concept of flexicurity rests on the assumption that flexibility and security are not contradictory, but complementary and even mutually supportive. It brings together a low level of protection of workers against dismissals with high unemployment benefits and a labour market policy based on an obligation and a right of the unemployed to training. The concept of 'job security' is replaced by 'employment security'. Social dialogue between employers and employees is an important aspect of the flexicurity model, which is developed in Scandinavian countries. For a discussion on the potential of the flexicurity model for other European countries see Conference 'Flexicurity on the labour market: are the EU-25 speaking the same language?' September 14th 2005, hosted by the European Policy Center, the Confederation of Danish Trade Unions, and the Confederation of Danish Employers.

Bibliography

Coetsier, P. (1966) An approach to the study of the attitudes of workers on conveyor belt assembly lines, in: *The International Journal of Production Research*, 5(2): 113–35.

Costa G. (1996) The impact of shift and night work on health, in: *Applied Ergonomics*, 27(1): 9–16.

Daems, H. (1990) Nationale verankering en concurentievermogen, in: *Tijdschrift Voor Economie en Management*, 35(1): 73–85.

Huys, R. and Van Hootegem, G. (1999) 'Volvo-Ghent: a third way?' in J.P. Durand, J.J. Castillo and P. Stewart (eds), *Teamwork in the automobile industry. Radical change or passing fashion?.* Houndmills: Macmillan, pp. 308–24.

Huys, R. (2001) *Uit de band? De structuur van arbeidsverdeling in de Belgische autoassemblagebedrijven,* Doctoraal proefschrift, Departement Sociologie-K.U. Leuven, Leuven, p. 445.

Huys, R. and Van Hootegem, G. (2004) The division of labour and its impact on learning at work, in: Fischer, M., Boreham, N. and Nyhan, B. (eds), *European perspectives on learning at work: the acquisition of work process knowledge,* Cedefop Reference Series 56, Office for Official Publication for the European Communities: Luxembourg, pp. 166–85.

Layan, J.-B. and Lung, Y. (1995) La globalisation de l'industrie automobile laisse-t-elle une place aux intégrations régionales périphériques? Le cas de l'industrie automobile, in: Célimene, F. Lacour, C. (eds), *L'intégration régionale des espaces.* Economica: Paris, pp. 255–70.

Lehndorff, S. (1991) *Arbeitszeiten und Betriebszeiten in der Europäischen Automobilindustrie.* Köln: Institut Arbeit und Technik.

Lehndorff, S. (1999) *Working time and operating hours in the European automotive industry.* Köln: Institut Arbeit und Technik.

Leys, C. (2001) *Market-Driven Politics. Neoliberal democracy and the public interest.* London: Verso Books.

Lung, Y. (2002) The changing geography of the European Automobile System, Paper presented at the tenth GERPISA International colloquium, *Co-ordinating competencies and knowledge in the auto industry,* Paris, 6–8 June 2002.

Pact van Vilvoorde (2001), URL:http://www.kleurrijkvlaanderen/doc/doel-stellingen.pdf

Riedmann, A. (2006) *European Establishment Survey on working time and work-life balance – Overview report.* München: TNS Infratest Sozialforschung.

Schumann, M., Kuhlmann, M., Sanders, F. and Sperling, H.-J. (hrsg.) (2006) *Auto 5000: ein neues Produktionskonzept. Die deutsche Antwort auf Toyota?.* Hamburg: VSA.

Totterdill, P., Dhondt, S. and Milsone, S. (2002) *Partners at work? A report to Europe's policy makers and social partners.* Nottingham: University of Nottingham.

Vanhulle, S. and Van Gorp, T. (1997) *Na Renault is niemand nog veilig.* Berchem: EPO.

Womack, J.P., Jones, D.T. and Roos, D. (1990) *The machine that changed the world.* New York: Rawson Associates.

5
From Lean Production to Mass Customisation: Recent Developments in the Australian Automotive Industry

Richard Cooney and Graham Sewell

Introduction

Given its relatively marginal status as a manufacturing economy it may come as a surprise to learn that Australia has a well established and highly internationalised automotive manufacturing industry dominated by leading US and Japanese corporations. Automotive manufacturing began early in Australia with the Ford Motor Company commencing full local manufacturing in 1928, to be followed by General Motors-Holden in 1949, Mitsubishi in 1977 and Toyota in 1979. The more recently arrived Japanese manufacturers have been known to refer to the Australian vehicle industry as a 'bonsai' industry; small but well-developed in all its detail. This bonsai industry is hardly thriving, with Australia accounting for less than 0.5 per cent of annual global vehicle production, but is, nevertheless, striving to cope with the rigours of globalisation.

This struggle of Australian manufacturers to find an organisation of production that will be effective in global markets has seen the Australian industry subjected to continuous reform and restructuring over the course of the past two decades. Government policies and the automotive firms' global requirements have changed, along with the business strategies of local subsidiaries. The repositioning of local subsidiary firms in response to globalisation has seen them adopt differing approaches to the implementation of lean production practices, leading to some important differences in their reorganised systems of production. The idea promoted by books such as *The Machine That Changed The World* of a convergence towards the lean model of productive organisation is belied by the reality of the Australian automotive industry, even when, *prima facie*, the Australian industry would be an obvious candidate for convergence towards a single model of production. Indeed, Womack *et al.* (1990) marked it out as the country with a highly developed industry that was most in need of the benefits of lean production. In this respect the Australian auto industry makes an interesting test case, not so much of whether lean production has been a success or failure in a narrow economic sense but rather of whether lean has become the new model of production organisation.

In this chapter we examine the recent developments in the Australian automotive industry. The chapter outlines two eras of industry reform; an era of state sponsorship of lean production, followed by an era of deregulation and diversification in production organisations. To highlight the diversity of these organisations of production we focus upon the two most divergent examples of the adoption of lean practice, those of Toyota Motor Corporation of Australia (TMCA) and Ford of Australia (FOA). These two firms exhibit different profit strategies underpinned by different product policies and different forms of the organisation of production (Boyer and Freyssenet, 2000). Toyota has followed the path of lean production in its organisation of production and has developed a work organisation based upon the functional flexibility of employees, whilst Ford has adapted lean production practice to develop an organisation of production based upon mass customisation. This organisation of production is allied to forms of work organisation based upon the product flexibility of employees. These differences in the deployment of labour in the production organisation are, we argue, related to the different ways in which the reintegration of conception and execution has been undertaken within the two firms during the reform process. Different rubrics of integration have developed to tap the discretionary effort of employees, as these firms restructure themselves to face the rigours of survival in the global automotive marketplace.

This chapter highlights the diversity of production organisations in the Australian automotive industry, challenging the idea of a global convergence towards a monolithic model of lean production, even in what effectively is a peripheral player in the international automotive industry.

The reintegration of conception and execution

The new production organisations in Australia have all sought to break with the previously Fordist organisation of production. As Boyer and Durand (1997) acknowledge, working 'flat out' in order to maximise output under a nominally Fordist productive regime can be counter-productive. Where competitive advantage is sought through improvements in product quality or product/process innovation, the appropriation of employees' discretionary mental labour becomes as important as the appropriation of their physical labour and the reliance upon one without the other many become counter-productive.

In the case of lean production, one of the key developments at the heart of the organisation of production is the dissolution of the separation of conception and execution through the implementation of teamwork (Cooney, 2004; Sewell, 1998). Although they engage in surprisingly little discussion of employment relations or labour management, either before or after the implementation of lean production, Womack *et al.* (1990) return to what has been seen since the late 19th century as the 'Man Problem' or 'Labour Problem' – i.e. the stultifying boredom of unskilled work (Noble, 1979). For the proponents of lean production this still remains the main cause of employee discontent and turnover under conditions of mass production. Their view of the labour problem does not, however, reflect the common dichotomisation between the relentless pursuit of efficiency at all costs associated with mass production (where employees are simply a factor of production to be rationality controlled) and the humanising effects of teamwork (where employees are normatively integrated into the corporation). Rather, under the rubric of lean production, Womack *et al.* (1990) are seeking to combine:

> ... the advantages of craft and mass production, while avoiding the high cost of the former and the rigidity of the latter. Toward this end, lean producers employ teams of multi-skilled workers at all levels of the organization and use highly flexible, increasingly automated machines to produce volumes of products in enormous quantities (Womack *et al.*, 1990: 13).

Rather than being a radical departure from previous management practice, this hedging between the normative and the rational on the part of Womack *et al.*, reflects a tradition – exemplified by the Human Relations School – that attempts to reconcile the increased routinisation of large-scale enterprises with the desire to reduce monotony and alienation by safeguarding employee discretion (Bendix, 1956). Barley and Kunda (1992) have previously argued that these tendencies map onto enduring rational and normative rhetorics of control that have ebbed and flowed in the management literature over the last 120 years. In turn, these rhetorics reflect fundamental beliefs about 'organic' and 'mechanistic' solidarity respectively (cf. Durkheim 1984) – what Barley and Kunda identify as the main 'cultural antinomies' of modernity. With this in mind, they attempt to demonstrate empirically the '... tendency for innovative surges of managerial theorizing to alternate between rational and normative rhetorics of control' (Barley and Kunda, 1992: 363). While we agree with Barley and Kunda's contention that 'mechanical' (to use Durkheim's own phrase) and 'organic' solidarity stand in a logically antinomian relationship to each other, based on our foregoing discussion we would counter that it is difficult to place lean production wholly in one or the other of these discrete categories. However, the concept of a set of cultural antinomies does allow us to make sense of the differing applications of lean practices in different production organisations.

The starting point for understanding variation in the application of lean practices is Durkheim's (1984) belief that mechanical and organic solidarity constituted pre-modern and modern ideals of social cohesion respectively. This is consistent with the representation of teamwork as being either a more efficient form of production organisation or a reversion to a more natural form of work organisation after the anomalous interruption of an industrial division of labour based on a rigid separation of conception and execution (Sewell, 2001). Thus, although lean production displays rational and normative characteristics simultaneously, the degree to which an organisation sees mechanical or organic solidarity as being the primary basis of its social cohesion will lead it to place particular emphasis on either rational or normative forms of control. This is not to say, as Barley and Kunda also acknowledge, that this is a mutually exclusive relationship and that rational and normative forms of control cannot coexist. Rather, it is that when an organisation is confident that relations of mechanical solidarity are already in place, then it is provided with the sufficient level of ontological security to place its focus on rational forms of control and vice versa. Interestingly, in one key passage Womack *et al.* (1990) allude to this very point. It starts with an expression of surprise that Ford in the US – a company that they observe had not fundamentally changed in industrial relations practices since 1938 – had been particularly adept at embracing teamwork and reaping the productive benefits of increased employee discretion. In contrast, General Motors' US plants – a company often perceived to be ahead of Ford in terms of the implementation of innovative employment practices – were still struggling to implement teamwork effectively and improve employee morale eroded though a long standing program of plant closures. Their explanation for this apparent contradiction is consistent with our contention in as much as Womack *et al.* (1990) attributed Ford's success to the widespread belief amongst employees that managers had mastered the technical aspects of lean production to such an extent that the whole corporation was able to focus on the pursuit of mutual goals. In contrast, GM's failure to grasp the 'hard' aspects of lean production meant that it had little time to focus on 'softer' matters such as normative integration. This particular failure of GM is borne out by Adler's (1993) detailed discussion of the experience of NUMMI, the former GM Fremont plant effectively taken over by Toyota as a test bed for its production system in the US. Toyota's confidence in and mastery of the rational aspects of lean production allowed it to concentrate its managerial efforts on practices of normative integration at NUMMI that emphasised mutual dependency, an observation also confirmed by Besser's (1995) study of Toyota's Kentucky plant.

Before we go on to the empirical component of our chapter we want to introduce an important qualification to the foregoing discussion. We are anxious to establish that we do not see mechanical and organic solidarity as organisational states that necessarily signal the presence of normative or rational managerial control respectively. Rather, it is our view that these types of binary opposition are figurative elements of a long running debate that circulates around beliefs about the desirability of consent and coercion in social relations – for example, Hobbes' 'Leviathan' versus Rousseau's 'State of Nature' right up to discussion of the rigidities of mass production and the autonomy of craft production contained in Womack *et al.*

(1990) – rather than literal representations of material processes of society. It is also our view that Barley and Kunda do not make this important distinction clear enough and, as a result, we are cautious of representing Australian industrial history in such potentially functionalist terms. Thus, we would re-emphasise that we are using their definitions of 'rational' and 'normative' integration as taxonomic, rather than theoretical, categories that help us to convey how Australian auto manufacturers interpret the lean production model and use it to legitimate certain practices.

The Australian vehicle industry

Australia has a long history of automotive manufacture with the Ford Motor Company commencing local assembly of the Model-T in 1925. Local manufacturing began in 1928 when Ford opened a purpose built factory at Geelong – the first Ford plant built outside of North America – to produce the Model-A (Ford Motor Company n.d.). Whilst the locally manufactured Ford vehicles introduced innovations such as the utility body, the first Australian designed vehicle did not appear until 1948 when General Motors commenced manufacture of the first Holden. General Motors had entered the local industry in 1935 through the acquisition of the local vehicle body builder Holden, but it commenced an assembly only operation and local manufacturing did not begin until after the end of the Second World War (Davidson and Stewardson, 1975). The second locally designed vehicle went into production in 1963 when the first of the Ford Falcon range appeared. With the shift of GM-Holden to global vehicle designs in the 1980's, the Falcon range remains the only fully Australian designed vehicle range in production. Australian vehicle manufacturers tried unsuccessfully (Hartnett, 1964) to enter the industry but it continued to be dominated by the two big US firms and there was little change in the Fordist structure of the industry until Japanese manufacturers such as Toyota, Mitsubishi and Nissan entered local manufacturing in the mid-1970s (Edgington, 1990).

The Fordist structure of the industry, where two US firms dominated a small industry focused upon domestic production, began to unravel in the 1980s. The arrival of the Japanese and changes in Australian government policy towards the industry, led to a dramatic restructuring. The Australian state took upon itself the nation building task of reforming the industry and integrating it with the new networks of global accumulation. In 1985 the industry was protected by tariffs (57.5 per cent) and import quotas (110,000 vehicles). Five vehicle manufacturers produced 13 different models with average production runs of less than 30,000 vehicles (Automotive Industry Authority, 1986). The government sought to restructure the industry by removing quotas and progressively reducing tariffs. The government car plan sought to internationalise the industry by: a) encouraging the development of an export focus amongst vehicle and component manufacturers through the use of export incentive schemes, b) reducing model numbers through cooperation amongst manufacturers and the cross-badging of vehicles, c) increasing average production volumes to 100,000 vehicles and, d) reforming employee relations practices to encourage the adoption of new work methods and new production practices (Automotive Industry Authority, 1987).

The first phase of reform

The first era of reform from 1985 to 1995 was marked by the promotion of lean production practices through a bipartite approach to change. Government programs promoted the use of workplace consultative mechanisms in conjunction with the introduction of lean production practices under the umbrella of an industry best practice program. These activities were supported by a government plan for the industry. The Toyota Production System (TPS) was promoted as the model of best practice at this time and the adoption of practices from the TPS was seen as key to the future survival of the Australian industry.

The implementation of the new policies led to the spatial reorganisation of the industry. The reduction in the number of models in production led to the closure of plants by the US firms and an investment in new production facilities by the Japanese firms. Ford and GM-Holden both closed plants and concentrated their vehicle assembly operations on a single site whilst Toyota invested in new single-site facilities (Automotive Industry Authority, 1987).

The vehicle producers' rationalisation of their production facilities was followed by the restructuring of their supplier networks. The vehicle producers implemented just-in-time delivery, transferred responsibility for quality to suppliers, implemented cost-down policies and began to single source components (Berggren, 1992; Jureidini, 1991; Sohal, 1991). The Toyota Motor Corporation, for example, was able to reduce its supplier base from 300 firms in 1988 to 100 firms in 1994 through the implementation of such policies (Langfield-Smith and Greenwood, 1998: 338). Whilst not moving to modular factory organisations, the vehicle producers did focus their activities on vehicle design and body building with Ford, for example, selling off the plastics plant at their Broadmeadows site to Venture Plastics, a multinational US component firm.

The shake-out in the component industry led to the closure of component manufacturing plants and the break-up of long established Australian component manufacturing groups such as the Hendersons group, but it also led to new investment in the sector as the US firms outsourced more of their component manufacture (Lynch, 1996) and the Japanese established new joint venture firms. The component sector was increasingly being integrated into global supply chains as large multinational component firms entered the Australian industry (Berggren, 1992).

This restructuring of the industry was driven through the extensive use of bipartite government-industry bodies and tripartite government-industry-union bodies (Bramble, 1993; Jureidini, 1991), a process which was widely criticised at the time for its corporatist orientation (Beilharz, 1994; Stilwell, 1986). Policy directions were agreed in tripartite forums involving government and peak bodies such as the Australian Council of Trade Unions and the Metal Trades Industry Association, with little involvement of the employers and local union officials that were to implement them.

The second phase of reform

The most recent developments in the industry, those of the second era from 1995–2005, have been marked by the reverse of the policies followed in the first era. The second era has been marked by government policies of industry deregulation and this has opened up a space for the manufacturers to implement their own customised suites of management practices allied to differing business strategies. The attempt of the state to impose the Toyota model through a process of industry planning in the first phase faltered and was followed by a phase of deregulation.

Workplace consultative bodies have declined in the second era and industry consultative bodies have been abolished. The deregulation of industrial relations in this era has also seen the growth of plants with workers on individual contracts amongst the component producers and the spread of individualised workplace relations has been supported by the major firms in the industry (Hawke and Woden, 1999).

The components industry has been further concentrated with 12 large multinational first tier suppliers at the head of a sector that now contains only 200 firms in total. Many of these firms are being squeezed by the automotive producers – especially the US firms – who prefer more contractual relationships with suppliers rather than long-term partnerships following the lean model. This has led to another crisis in the automotive supplier industry, with Australian suppliers being under continuous cost pressure and the threat of substitution from suppliers in Asia. The automotive industry supply chain thus evidences two different models in Australia. On the one hand is the lean model where close relationships with local suppliers are used to achieve continuing cost reductions, on the other hand is the customisation model where the supply chain is segmented between imported basic components and local finishing or customisation of complete vehicle systems. Under the latter model, a small number of first tier suppliers customise vehicle systems (e.g. interior systems, power trains, etc.) and provide synchronous supply or in-line sequencing of complete modules to line side in the vehicle manufacturing firms. The second period of reform has thus seen the increasing development of component modularisation, especially where this involves higher levels of customisation (Singh, Smith and Sohal, 2003; Productivity Commission, 2002).

The second era has been characterised by the implementation of producer's global production systems. The North American producers in Australia, GM-Holden and Ford, have developed their own standardised global production systems and these have been deployed in their Australian operations. These systems have incorporated lean practices within them but diverge from the Toyota model in certain critical respects. Firstly, the Ford Production System promotes European style group working practices supported by training and skill-based pay. Ford has also sought to create partnership relations with the automotive union. The GM Global Production System is closer to the Toyota system but promotes greater flexibility in plant operations. These systems have been used in Australia to develop an organisation of production for the mass customisation of auto-mobiles. The North American producers manufacture a much greater variety of vehicles in Australia than does Toyota and they have created producer networks for vehicle customisation alongside their lean supply chains. Mass customisation strategies have been the basis for survival of these firms as they seek to compete with the Japanese firms – Toyota and Mitsubishi – in Australia.

Divergent approaches to productive organisation

The failure of the attempted convergence on lean production practice in the first era of reform has highlighted the divergence of production organisations in the era of deregulation. The restructuring of work practices and employment relations within the vehicle manufacturing firms has taken some very different paths, as has the introduction of lean production practices such as just-in-time (JIT) and total quality control (TQC).

The vehicle producers and component manufacturers have implemented JIT supply but this did not mean that they had all implemented internal JIT systems. The implementation of JIT control methods varied with firms using batch systems, manufacturing resource planning systems and hybrid push-pull systems (Cooney, 2002; Sohal, Ramsay and Samson, 1993). Not all firms used visual control methods such as Kanban boards, Heijunka posts and Andon boards. Only five of the 30 manufacturing firms surveyed by Sohal, Ramsay and Samson (1993), for example, had introduced Kanban systems.

Methods to increase the mobility of capital, to improve cash flows and reduce fixed capital, were widely implemented but this was not always associated with the full implementation of just-in-time (Sohal, 1991). The disciplinary controls of JIT (Sewell, 1998) were not essential where normative control methods were used and these two aspects of JIT (the disciplinary control of labour and the improvement of capital mobility) should be viewed separately. They are combined in the lean model but have been disarticulated in other models.

The use of JIT was adapted to different ends in different firms but value-adding process redesign methods of cellularisation were more widely used. The US firms (Dawson, 1994; Mathews, 1994) and leading component manufacturers (Langfield-Smith and Greenwood, 1998; Nichol and Sunderman, 1993; Sohal, Ramsay and Samson, 1993) adopted cellular plant lay-outs and introduced cycle-time reduction techniques such as lot size reduction, quick tooling changeovers and stock reduction.

These efforts to improve the efficiency of production were complemented by efforts to improve the quality of cars and components. Quality control methods were widely disseminated but once again there were differences between the more normatively oriented approaches to quality management and the more rationally oriented approaches. In this case, in fact, these differences resulted in the institutional separation of the peak quality bodies in Australia with the Australian Quality Council (AQC) promoting employee involvement and organisational culture change along with the implementation of specific control techniques (Dawson and Palmer, 1995) whilst the Australian Organization for Quality (AOQ) focused almost exclusively on control systems engineering and quality certification (Nettle, 1990).

The vehicle manufacturers all produced their own standards for supplier certification and also required suppliers to achieve ISO 9000 certification but beyond this, enterprise managements exercised discretion about the methods of quality management used in individual enterprises. The use of the broader organisational change elements that were promoted by the AQC varied from firm to firm. The implementation of process control techniques was mandatory but the ways in which continuous improvement and employee involvement were implemented were decisions for the individual firm. Some firms opted for a limited expansion of employees' work role – introducing some responsibility for housekeeping and routine maintenance, for example – whilst others opted for a more thorough going reintegration of tasks covering problem solving, quality control, equipments set-ups, and so on. Firms also adopted different sets of teamwork practices to implement quality improvements. Some made minimal use of teamwork using small off-line groups to work solely on performance improvement activities, whilst others used a variety of teams including on-line teams to improve quality and safety in the work environment. These latter teams offered greater scope for the exercise of employee discretion and were usually associated with a greater scope of team responsibility. The preference for the integration of team responsibilities or for functional separation between production teams and problem solving teams reflected the relative emphasis that was placed on the use of rational or normative methods of integration by different producers. Producers, such as Toyota, undertook problem-solving and continuous improvement activities in separate specialised groups using work area groups to communicate with management and establishing specialised off-line groups such as Quality Circles to undertake problem-solving activities, whilst others, such as Ford, used integrated, on-line work teams that both improved performance and the safety of the work environment (Cooney and Sohal, 2004; Gough, MacIntosh and Park, 2006; Park, Erwin and Knapp, 1997).

The different adoption of just-in-time, quality management and teamworking reflected the different emphasis placed on the rational or normative integration of conception and execution by different firms. This is further in evidence when we consider the differing approaches to the management of employee relations at the leading vehicle manufacturers. In the mid-1980s, at the beginning of the industry reform process, the auto manufacturers in Australia sought to reform the conflictual industrial relationships that existed in the industry between management and industry unions (Bramble, 1993, 1996). Long strikes at Ford (Lever-Tracy, 1990) and at many of the component suppliers had given the industry a poor industrial relations record and with the support of government, the industry set about improving this record. Enterprise level consultative bodies were widely established (Marchington, 1992) and the industry began to implement employee involvement programs. These latter programs varied widely in their design however. The North American producers, Ford and GM-Holden, who had established 'Quality of Worklife' programs, sought direct, on-the-job forms of employee involvement, where all employees in a work area were involved in communicative, decision-making and problem solving activities whilst other producers, notably the Japanese, used more limited means of consultation such as suggestion schemes and brief employee communication meetings (Bramble, 1993; Simmons and Lansbury, 1996; Wilkinson, 1988).

The adoption of lean practices and the reform of employment relations thus shows a continuing divergence in the organisation of production between the US and Japanese vehicle producers in Australia. We now turn to a more detailed comparison of Ford and Toyota to highlight that divergence. This comparison is based upon interviews with corporate managers and a comparative study of the body plants at Ford and Toyota. In each plant production managers and HR managers were interviewed, along with the work team leaders. In total 68 semi-structured interviews were undertaken ranging in duration from 20 to 40 minutes.

Reform at Ford of Australia – normative integration and mass customisation

Ford Australia is the third largest of the Australian producers with a market share of around 17 per cent in 2005 placing it behind GM-Holden (21 per cent) and Toyota (22 per cent). Ford is unique in the Australian industry, being the only firm to design and develop products solely for the domestic market. GM-Holden customises global designs for its locally manufactured products, whilst the bulk of Toyota's production is of the Japanese designed Camry.

Ford designs and manufactures the Falcon range of products in Australia – five different body styles: a sedan, long wheel base sedan, estate wagon, body style utility, cab chassis utility – and in 2004 introduced the Ford Territory SUV range which is also designed and developed in Australia. Ford produces primarily for the domestic market – it produces no left hand drive vehicles – and has a small export program to the neighbouring countries such as New Zealand and South Africa. With its focus on the domestic market, Ford follows a mass customisation strategy where most vehicle types have high end derivatives that feature high performance and high design features. After faltering sales with its AU models, the company returned to profitability on the back of this strategy. The mix of highly customised vehicles went from under 10 per cent of sales with the AU models to over 30 per cent with the successor BA models.

Ford runs a large, variable batch production system for the manufacture of components internally (e.g. body panels) allied to the synchronous supply of modules at final assembly. Customisation thus occurs late in the production process, at final assembly or, indeed, in one of Ford's partner firms that customise vehicles after manufacture. This flexible factory approach stands in contrast to the focused factory using standardised batch sizes established by Toyota. Ford has thus eschewed the rationalisation of batch sizes favoured by Toyota and techniques such as JIT have had a different application. Stocks were reduced at Ford by implementing JIT supply and JIT delivery but there has been limited use of internal JIT in the reformed production process.

This organisation of production with its high product variety is allied to a work organisation based upon Natural Work Groups (NWGs). These work area groups undertake a range of production functions but the focus is upon the ability of the groups to produce a wide range of products and to multi-skill group members. All Ford vehicles are produced on the one assembly line and so the product flexibility of employees in each work area is critical to the final quality of the vehicle. The NWGs also have responsibility for problem solving and continuous improvement. They have a weekly 30 minute meeting – and the production line is stopped for these meetings – to work on work area issues. The NWGs can work on five open issues at any one time and these issues may be quality related, productivity related or work safety related. The issues cover matters current in the work area but the NWGs are also involved in new product development and introduction and hence some issues may be preventative ones related to future work. The Natural Work Groups at Ford are larger and more heterogeneous in composition than comparable work teams at Toyota and they meet more regularly and for much longer than do comparable groups at Toyota. The NWGs are the base unit of the organisational structure and as such are delegated greater autonomy than are comparable groups at Toyota. Employees at Ford, for example, participate in the election of their own group leaders, whilst all team leaders at Toyota are appointed by management (Cooney, 1999; Cooney and Sohal, 2004; Simmons and Lansbury, 1996).

The reintegration of conception and execution at Ford Australia to deliver high levels of product customisation has focused upon normative integration and the development of a strong company culture. Ford Australia had a history of poor industrial relations and had experienced several bitter strikes during the 1970s – the longest of which went for ten weeks. Although the firm subsequently won Australian Quality Awards in the 1980s and 1990s, there were fears that the productivity gains achieved through these efforts would be undermined by industrial disruption. Thus, the development of a new organisation of production at Ford was seen as providing the opportunity to consolidate quality achievements by addressing the perceived failure of the mass production techniques to support mechanistic forms of solidarity within the firm. Employees were to be recognised as the foundation of Ford's success. Moreover, this was a message for internal and external consumption; corporate advertising in Australia in the 1990s promoted not the Ford product but the Ford people, people who are so committed to their work that, in the words of the advertising slogan, they 'Live It.' Ford makes a great investment in what it sees as 'people' related activities. Ford provides an internal career structure for employees that reaches from operator level to middle management, with company sponsored training and qualifications available at each step along the way. Ford provides significantly more training than other firms in the industry and led the industry in the introduction of vocational qualifications for all its employees (Cooney, 1997).

The development of the Natural Work Groups at Ford has been one of the cornerstones of the normative integration of conception and execution in the new organisation of production. The extent of the discretion delegated to employees means that these groups have outcomes for both employees and the company. These work groups follow the high road (Bacon and Blyton, 2000) of work design where the pursuit of quality and productivity gains is not at the expense of safety in the work environment.

The orientation towards employees, the development of group life and group working is evident from our interviews with Natural Work Group Leaders at Ford. The NWG Leaders see benefits for both their group members and the company in the Ford work organisation:

> The guys have an input to safety and we work out how to make the jobs run better. I might have one idea and the group has another idea but we work it out together and come up with the best idea. The guys know their job and work together well. They are not line operators who just come in to do their job, get their pay every week and go home. (Angelo – Ford NWG Leader)

The thing I like about them [NWGs] is that people have a chance to take an interest in the job and come up with ideas. They have the opportunity to say something and to make the job easier for themselves and that's a positive, to have the feeling of doing something for yourself rather than having it all done for you. (Bob – Ford NWG Group Leader)

The satisfaction derived from the group leader's role also comes from the development of group life:

... I like to see my group working as a group which gives me satisfaction. Issues are raised in meetings and we start to work on them and become enthusiastic about them. That's important because issues are what we want. They are important to the people and important to the job itself because they improve the group and they improve the job. (Paul – Ford NWG Leader)

The development of a new organisation of production at Ford Australia has been characterised by an emphasis upon the reorganisation of work and employee orientations towards work, in advance of the application of an instrumental rationality to the reorganisation of production. The rationalisation of production methods has been overshadowed by a managerial embrace of those aspects of lean production that resonate with the development of Ford people and Ford values. The company that once boasted a Sociological Department now seeks the pursuit of mechanistic solidarity through the reorganisation of work around teams. Here Ford's use of the term *Natural* Work Group is instructive, instilling a belief that teamwork is closer to some natural human state of cooperative effort (Sewell, 2001). For Ford, the search for mechanistic solidarity has influenced the reception of lean production in Australia. The new organisation of production has provided Ford with a counterpoint to the pursuit of organic solidarity under the mass production regime and it has facilitated the reinvention of mass production as mass customisation where the provision of greater value-added services to the customer is predicated upon the normative orientation of employees to the new mission of the corporation.

Reform at Toyota Motor Corporation of Australia – rational integration and lean production

The Toyota Motor Corporation of Australia (TMCA) is the country's leading vehicle company. Toyota has the largest domestic market share of any automotive company and it is also the largest exporter of cars from Australia. Toyota manufactures a limited range of products in Australia – just two standard sedans (medium and large). Most production is of the medium sedan which is made in a left hand drive variant for export. Export sales are very important for Toyota Australia as they account for 40 per cent of local production. Despite its pre-eminent position in the Australian market, however, TMCA has not been consistently profitable and hence has been under continuing pressure to reduce costs.

Toyota produces no high end derivative vehicles from its range; rather, its business strategy is centered on the continuous improvement of quality and the continuous reduction of cost for a limited range of standard vehicles. Toyota has carried out the most extensive rationalisation of its supplier network (Langfield-Smith and Greenwood, 1998) and has extensively implemented JIT in its plants, with batch sizes and manufacturing cycle times being heavily standardised. The system is controlled by management through the use of kanban and surveillance techniques such as andon boards. Indeed, managers have their own mini-andon boards in their offices to monitor the state of the line. Quality controls such as Statistical Process Control are also extensively implemented with the concomitant standardisation of machine settings and work tasks. The rational control of all aspects of the production system – machines, tools and employee tasks – is in the ascendant at Toyota, whilst there is less emphasis on employee development and normative integration through teamwork.

Toyota offers only short career ladders in comparison to Ford, with career progression only being applied within the band – e.g. operators can only realistically expect to remain as operators. Toyota has fewer employee training programs and there is also an instrumental approach to teamworking. The teams at Toyota are focused upon direct production or value-adding activities and have only a communicative function where employees are concerned – i.e. they are a mechanism for management to communicate information about production to employees. The production teams at Toyota are small, homogenous and rarely have meetings. They only undertake production tasks, as safety, problem-solving and continuous improvement activities are undertaken by off-line Quality Circles and Goshi Teams. There are few of these Quality Circle groups and Goshi Teams, involving only small numbers of employees in activities beyond those associated with direct production work.

The organisation of production at Toyota thus features a rational integration of conception and execution to deliver low costs based upon a functional separation of tasks (e.g. production and continuous improvement). The production teams at Toyota feature a low road approach to work design with a focus upon performance outcomes only. Employees exhibit functional flexibility as they have a standard range of products to work on, but are expected to rotate across work areas to balance production. These rotations are primarily for operational reasons and few employees rotate into Quality Circles and Goshi Teams.

Further evidence of the instrumental rationalisation of work at Toyota can be found in the following interviews with production team leaders. Their orientation is towards the performance of the work area rather than the development of group life.

> The important thing is to make panels on-time, give delivery on-time and quality. ... I've got to answer to the group leader when there's a problem. I have to explain to him why we broke a die or why we don't have panels. (Sally – Toyota Production Team Leader)

> The challenge is to produce panels with quality. We have some problems at the moment with some jobs, so we get maintenance and the toolmakers involved with the job and see if we can solve those problems. (Enrico – Toyota Production Team Leader)

The team leader role at Toyota is also seen in instrumental terms – explaining production requirements to employees:

> They're a good bunch but I'm always explaining things, why, why, why. Most have been here for a while so they understand and the new ones, I just answer their questions. They have prob-

lems but not big ones, little bicky ones. They usually get over it or I say 'I don't know' I'm good at explaining stuff like that, why, why. I have twin boys at home so that's where I've developed the talent. Instead of just telling, explain why. (June – Toyota Production Team Leader)

The emphasis on normative integration in the new production organisation at Ford and the lower priority given to the rational-isation of the production system itself presents a mirror image of the development of lean production at Toyota. It is not that normative integration has never been a factor at Toyota; on the contrary, the development of Toyota Australia has always been predicated upon the transfer of 'best practice' techniques from the Japanese parent to the Australian subsidiary to counter its perception that there was an 'Australian worker' problem. This normative integration is, however, taken-for-granted and so the focus is upon the instrumental transfer of new production techniques that have yet to be learnt in Australia. For TMCA the Toyota Production system is unquestionably 'best practice' and hence the emphasis is upon the rational mastery of that system in Australia. The company has interpreted the arrival of lean production in Australia as an opportunity to transfer the latest developments in the technical rationality of production to an under performing subsidiary company. Indeed, successive Presidents of Toyota Australia have emphasised the importance of improving performance to bring the corporation up to Japanese standards if continued investment in Australian facilities is to be ensured. Thus, the reception of lean production at Toyota Australia has brought to the fore the pursuit of organic solidarity through the application of best practice techniques premised on a narrow conception of instrumental rationalism and productive efficiency.

Conclusion

The development of diverse organisations of production in Australia represents something of a disappointment for those seeking evidence of a homogenous transformation wrought by an epoch-making model of lean production. Yes, the new practices and techniques associated with lean have been taken up by all Australian producers but no, this has not led to a convergence of either production practice or forms of work organisation. Despite sponsorship by the state, lean production has not emerged as *the* production paradigm for the Australian vehicle industry.

The transformation of the Australian industry in the past two decades does, however, show a reintegration of conception and execution in all organisations of production. Expanded job responsibilities, including involvement in problem solving and the continuous improvement of quality and productivity, have been common across the industry. How this reintegration has been undertaken has, however, varied greatly from company to company. Reintegration has been conditional upon the contrasting ideals about the nature of social cohesion and solidarity within different firms. At Ford, mechanistic solidarity has been seen to be at risk and so normative approaches to reintegration have been followed, whilst, at Toyota organic solidarity has been perceived to be at risk and so more rational approaches to reintegration have been followed.

The different rubrics of reintegration identified here are an important element of recent developments in the Australian automotive industry and examining the divergences in contemporary organisations of production without being able to account for the route travelled to those new organisations would, in our view, give a diminished account of recent events. The Australian experience thus provides some interesting case studies of the recent transformations in the automotive industry. These may be bonsai cases but they do reflect the divergence in production organisations and the divergent routes taken to them.

Bibliography

Adler, P. (1993) 'The "Learning Bureaucracy": New United Motor Manufacturing, Inc.', *Research in Organisational Behaviour*, vol. 15, pp. 111–94.

Automotive Industry Authority (1986) *Report on the State of the Automotive Industry 1985*. Canberra: Australian Government Publishing Service.

Automotive Industry Authority (1987) *Report on the State of the Automotive Industry 1986*. Canberra: Australian Government Publishing Service.

Barley, S.R. and Kunda, G. (1992) 'Design and Devotion: Surges of Rational and Normative Ideologies of Control in Managerial Discourse', *Administrative Science Quarterly*, vol. 37, no. 3, pp. 363–81.

Bacon, N. and Blyton, P. (2000) 'High Road and Low Road Teamworking: Perceptions of management rationales and organization and human resource outcomes', *Human Relations*, vol. 53, no. 11, pp. 1425–58.

Beilharz, P. (1994) *Transforming Labour. Labour Tradition and the Labor Decade in Australia.* Cambridge: Cambridge University Press.

Bendix, R. (1956) *Work and Authority in Industry: Ideologies of management in the course of industrialization.* New York: John Wiley.

Berggren, C. (1992) 'Changing Buyer-Supplier Relations in the Australian Automotive Industry. Innovative Partnerships or Intensified Control?', *Working Paper No. 25,* Sydney: Centre for Corporate Change, University of New South Wales.

Besser, T.L. (1995) 'Rewards and organizational goal achievement: A case study of Toyota Motor Manufacturing in Kentucky', *Journal of Management Studies,* vol. 32, no. 3, pp. 383–99.

Bramble, T.J. (1993) *The Contingent Conservatism of Full-Time Trade Union Officials: A Case Study of the Vehicle Builders Employees' Federation of Australia,* unpublished PhD Thesis. La Trobe University.

Bramble, T.J. (1996) 'Strategy in Context: The Impact of Changing Regulatory Regimes on Industrial Relations Management in the Australian Vehicle Industry', *Asia Pacific Journal of Human Resources,* vol. 34, no. 3, pp. 48–64.

Boyer, R. and Durand, J.P. (1997) *After Fordism.* London: Macmillan.

Boyer, R. and Freyssenet, M. (2000) *The Productive Models. The Conditions of Profitability.* Houndmills, Basingstoke: Palgrave Macmillan.

Cooney, R. (1997) 'Training Reform in the Australian automotive industry', *International Journal of Training and Development,* vol. 1, no. 4, pp. 259–70.

Cooney, R. (1999) *Group Work and New Production Practices in the Australian Passenger Motor Vehicle Manufacturing Industry,* unpublished PhD Thesis. University of Melbourne.

Cooney, R. (2002) 'Is "Lean" a Universal Production System? Batch Production in the Automotive Industry', *International Journal of Operations & Production Management,* vol. 22, no. 10, pp. 1130–47.

Cooney, R. (2004) 'Empowered Self-Management and the Design of Work Teams', *Personnel Review,* vol. 33, no. 6, pp. 677–92.

Cooney, R. and Sohal, A. (2004) 'Teamwork and Total Quality Management: a durable partnership', *Total Quality Management and Business Excellence,* vol. 15, no. 8, pp. 1131–42.

Dawson, P. (1994) *Organizational Change: A Processual Approach.* London: Paul Chapman Publishing.

Dawson, P. and Palmer, G. (1995) *Quality Management: the Theory and Practice of Implementing Change.* Melbourne: Longman.

Davidson, F.G. and Stewardson, B.R. (1975) *Economics and Australian Industry.* Hawthorn: Longman Australia.

Durkheim, E. (1984) *The division of labor in society.* New York: The Free Press.

Edgington, D.W. (1990) *Japanese Business Down Under. Patterns of Japanese Investment.* London: Routledge.

Gough, R., MacIntosh, M. and Park, B. (2006) 'The Influence of Decentralised Bargaining Systems on the Introduction of Continuous Improvement Practices in Australian Automotive Components Companies', *Asia Pacific Business Review,* vol. 12, no. 2, pp. 209–24.

Hartnett, L. (1964) *Big Wheels and Little Wheels*. Melbourne: Lansdowne Press.

Hawke, A. and Woden, M. (1999) 'The Changing Face of Australian Industrial Relations: A Survey', *The Economic Record*, vol. 74, no. 224, pp. 74–88.

Jureidini, R. (1991) 'Just-In-Time and Power Relations in the Manufacturing Chain', *Labour & Industry*, vol. 4, no. 1, pp. 23–40.

Langfield-Smith, K. and Greenwood, M. (1998) 'Developing Co-operative Buyer-Supplier Relationships: A case study of Toyota', *Journal of Management Studies*, vol. 35, no. 3, pp. 331–53.

Lever-Tracy, C. (1990) 'Fordism Transformed? Employee Involvement and workplace industrial relations at Ford', *The Journal of Industrial Relations*, vol. 33, no. 2, pp. 179–96.

Lynch, M. (1996) 'How Holden Beat the Odds', *The Age*, 12/6/96 p. 19.

Marchington, M. (1992) 'The Growth of Employee Involvement in Australia', *The Journal of Industrial Relations*, vol. 34, no. 5, pp. 472–81.

Mathews, J. (1994) *Catching The Wave. Workplace Reform In Australia*. New York: ILR Press, Ithaca.

Nettle, D. (1990) *Management Control in Australia: an historical perspective*, unpublished PhD. Thesis. Macquarie University.

Nichol, C. and Sunderman, F. (1993) 'Lean Operations at PBR', in *Developments in Automotive Manufacturing. Conference of the Society of Automotive Engineers. Australasia, 11/3/93*. Melbourne.

Noble, D. (1979) *The forces of production: A social history of industrial automation*. New York: Alfred Knopf.

Park, R., Erwin, P.J. and Knapp, K. (1997) 'Teams in Australia's automotive industry: Characteristics and future challenges', *The International Journal of Human Resource Management*, vol. 8, no. 6, pp. 780–96.

Productivity Commission (2002) *Review of Automotive Assistance. Inquiry Report No. 25*. Melbourne: Commonwealth of Australia.

Sewell, G. (1998) 'The discipline of teams: the control of team-based industrial work through electronic and peer surveillance', *Administrative Science Quarterly*, vol. 43, no. 2, pp. 397–428.

Sewell, G. (2001) 'What goes around, comes around: Inventing a mythology of teamwork and empowerment', *Journal of Applied Behavioral Science*, vol. 37, no. 1, pp. 70–89.

Simmons, D.E. and Lansbury, R.D. (1996) 'Worker Involvement at Ford Motor Company Australia', pp. 80–100 in Davis, E.E. and Lansbury, R.D. (eds), *Managing Together. Consultation and Participation in the Workplace*. Melbourne: Longman.

Singh, P.J., Smith, A. and Sohal, A. (2003) 'Strategic Supply Chain Management Issues in the Automotive Industry: an Australian perspective', *International Journal of Production Research*, vol. 43, no. 16, pp. 3375–99.

Sohal, A.S. (1991) 'Just-In-Time: Victorian Data', *Labour & Industry*, vol. 4, no. 1, pp. 41–54.

Sohal, A.S., Ramsay, L. and Samson, D. (1993) 'JIT Manufacturing: Industry Analysis and a Methodology for Implementation', *International Journal of Operations and Production Management*, vol. 13, no. 7, pp. 22–56.

Stilwell, F. (1986) *The Accord and Beyond. The Political Economy of the Labor Government*. Sydney: Pluto Press.

Wilkinson, R. (1988) 'Management strategies in the motor vehicle industry', pp. 128–41 in Willis, E. (ed.) *Technology and the Labour Process: Australasian Case Studies*. Sydney: Allen & Unwin.

Womack, J.P., Jones, D.T. and Roos, D. (1990) *The Machine that Changed the World: Based on the Massachusetts Institute of Technology 5-million dollar 5-year study on the future of the automobile*. New York: Rawson Associates.

6

Labour Relations in the Modular System: Ten Years of the VW Experience at Resende, Brazil

José Ricardo Ramalho and Elaine Marlova V. Francisco

Over the past ten years, Brazil's automotive industry has experienced important changes, triggered by the restructuring of its production sector worldwide. Initially, there was a significant upsurge in foreign direct investments allocated to new manufacturing plants from the mid-1990s onwards, establishing branches of all the main auto-assemblers in the country. Next, the companies decided to move away from the longest-established vehicle production area around São Paulo, instead opting for greenfield ventures in new regions. This was the context within which mature plants had to adapt to the flexibility criteria imposed by these new production strategies: these new plants were built in compliance with precepts of lean production, while workers and trade unions had to reorganise in order to deal with labour relations characterised by insecurity and new types of control on the factory floor.

The empirical reference point is the Volkswagen (VW) bus and lorry plant at Resende, in Rio de Janeiro State, inaugurated in 1996 which ushered in a new type of organisation of the production process known as the modular consortium. The purpose of this chapter[1] is to argue that recent developments in the vehicles industry – particularly in terms of worker-related management strategies – are neither innovative nor seamlessly aligned with a discourse calling for more worker participation in settling issues arising from the organisation of work. In fact, in terms of labour relations within the modular consortium, this new production system reproduces several characteristics of a traditional management model based on intensification of work, firm managerial control and low wages. However, once the VW Factory Committee[2] was set up as the in-house entity representing workers, we feel that it is possible to perceive new dimensions for worker and trade union participation within the plant, consequently introducing elements into a discussion of the build-up of new resistance practices. Information for this chapter was obtained through direct observation inside the plant, interviews and research on primary and secondary sources, between 2001 and 2003. Three in-depth interviews were conducted with members of the Factory Committee, five interviews with managers, four with shop-floor workers and two with local trade union officials. There was also an interview with VW's Latin American workers' representative in VW's World Workers Committee. Much of the discussion is based on a survey carried out in 2001, with the intention of establishing a profile of VW's workers in Resende. Other documents such as trade union bulletins, local newspapers and copies of collective agreements provided important source material.

Overview of industrial expansion in Brazil

Compared to the more industrialised nations, Brazil's automotive industry was a late starter back in the 1950s, when some foreign auto-assemblers built their first plants in the outskirts of the city of São Paulo. This developed into Brazil's main industrial hub, known as the ABC Region, encompassing the Santo André, São Bernardo and São Caetano districts that housed the main auto-assembly and auto components companies. Within this context, an import substitution policy developed that served as a springboard for this sector as a whole, particularly the auto components suppliers, many of them funded by Brazilian capital. On the labour side, this industrialisation process was the mainspring behind the development of a working class drawn largely from flows of migrants fleeing poverty-stricken rural areas, attracted by better jobs and more opportunities for social enhancement. Jobs in the automotive sector helped create a working class identity while firming up the organisational knowledge levels of these employees.

Production ballooned from 1950 to 1990, fuelled by the protectionist policies implemented by the Brazilian State, and also the vast growth of cities and other urban regions in Brazil. This situation began to change during the early 1990s, when the Federal Government introduced a deregulation policy that opened up the Brazilian market to global influences, with direct effects on this production chain. On the auto components supply side, there was a gradual but dramatic de-nationalisation in this sector, undermining the production experience built up over previous decades (cf. Abreu *et al.*, 1999). Among the auto-assemblers, a marked trend was noted towards restructuring the plants, but also and this might perhaps be almost unique to Brazil: the inflow of fresh investments, government incentives, respatialisation of new manufacturing plants seeking tax incentives, lower wages and weak trade unions, and the introduction of production strategies with innovative characteristics. The VW Plant at Resende was an advanced expression of this experimentation (cf. Abreu, Beynon and Ramalho, 2000), through which the suppliers were engaged in a joint venture with VW. The strategy was developed in order to create a modular system in which suppliers participated as partners in financing the plant and the organisation and assembly of the items in parallel units at the same site. This meant that VW no longer had workers in the assembly line, with its main tasks shifting to the production and sale of the vehicles.

One of the key reasons prompting the shift of the auto-assemblers to new locations is associated with a tax incentives policy established by the Brazilian Government, known the 'New Automotive Regime'.[3] This process triggered heated disputes among municipalities eager to attract investment. The effects of this policy varied, initially mirroring its predatory nature. According to Arbix *et al.* (1999) and Arbix (2000) these development strategies – which were presented as 'pro-active' – prompted disputes among States and Municipalities, with the only major loser being the public sector. This was somewhat ironic since the main reason for this engagement was the anticipated benefits to be reaped by local governments fortunate enough to attract large enterprises to their locality. Optimists believed success in this quest would be the spring board for broad economic development.

In the specific case of the Resende Municipality, where the modular consortium plant was established by VW, the upsurge in economic activity is evident. However, there have been other consequences as well, resulting in the formation of a better-educated labour force, able to establish a working class with its own identity. General data covering the period from 1995 through 2001 collated by the entities in charge of the industrial development of Rio de Janeiro State disclose that the Mid-Paraíba Region (which includes Resende) absorbed US$ 1 billion in private investment, generating 9,200 direct jobs, behind only the Rio de Janeiro State capital (*Gazeta Mercantil*, Rio de Janeiro, April 9, 2001, p. 1-b).

The VW modular consortium

One of the first of the auto-assemblers to allocate fresh investments, VW benefited from the tax incentives and low wages in this region. As mentioned in an earlier article (cf. Abreu, Beynon and Ramalho, 2000), the construction of the plant absorbed some US$ 300 million, part of which came from the companies constituting the modular consortium. This consisted of a group of seven sub-contractors in charge of the entire assembly line (chassis: Iochpe-Maxion; suspension and axles: Meritor; wheels and tyres: Remon; motors: Powertrain (joint venture between MWM and Cummings); cabs: Siemens-VDO; die-stamping: AKC (joint venture between Karmann Ghia and Aetra); and paintwork: Carese). The function of these companies is to share the responsibility for supplying the parts and handling the final assembly of the vehicles. At plants with production lines running on the Fordist system, the role of the suppliers was essentially to produce parts. A significant change occurred through the modular consortium, which altered the concept of the supplier network, bringing them into the plant as assemblers. But if these production arrangements were based on cooperative efforts among all those involved, and to a certain extent offset the downside of coordinating arrangements among different companies, the companies nevertheless remained separate legal entities that are juridically independent. As a result, the factory floor of this new plant had to be divided into separate 'segments', which allowed the companies to have their own addresses and legal identities.

Through this experiment, the VW auto-assembler remained outside the direct production process, focusing its attention on strategic functions such as vehicle design and architecture, as well as product policies, quality, marketing and sales. However, in this system, the auto-assembler cannot simply ignore the production side. It must develop a specific organisational capacity that allows it to integrate a group of supplier companies – now co-producers – in the manufacturing plant. To do so, VW had to build up an articulated administrative organisation concerned with monitoring production flows. This raises the issue of the nature of the relationship between the auto-assembler and its suppliers, both legally and in the Resende Plant.

The outcome of this process is that still today, each company in the 'consortium', organises its production in compliance with the targets set by Volkswagen, but does so individually, with the same applying to its logistics, work force recruitment and In-House Accident Prevention Commission (CIPA).[4] Although some modules may opt for multifunctional workers and cells, this is not a decision taken by the 'consortium', nor even a policy, but rather an individual strategy adopted by each business unit.

It is important to stress, that, in addition to the companies that constitute the modular consortium, production at this plant encompasses countless outsourced enterprises whose activities are not related to the production line (restaurant, cleaning, maintenance, security) as well as inside the plant, working with the modules, and totalling one half of the work force. All employees and outsourced workers[5] belong to the same Trade Union, but the collective agreements on wage adjustments, benefits and profits and earnings sharing are exclusive to workers employed by the companies in the modular consortium, excluding the employees of the outsourced companies. All consortium workers wear the same uniform (distinguished only by company logos), eat in the same restaurant and enjoy the same incentives and benefits policy. In terms of labour relations, the modular system frees the auto-assembler from the daily problems that crop up on the factory floor, although does not release it from participating in the negotiations and concessions offered to the workers, particularly because a system based so strongly on modular organisation cannot allow its activities to pause, as this would bring the entire production process to a halt.

Ten years after its implementation, the modular consortium currently features some significant alterations, including: the cab module partner was changed (the Brazilian cab manufacturer, Delga was replaced by AKC, which is a joint venture between Germany's Karmann Ghia, and Aetra, a Brazilian die-stamping company); a significant increase in the number of workers, employed by the 'consortium' as well as by the outsourced companies; and also the addition of an extra production shift. Through to 2004, the modular consortium had some 2,000 workers: 1,000 outsourced, 300 employed by VW and 700 working for by the partners. In 2005, there was a 35 per cent increase in the work force, reaching a total of 2,800, of whom 1,400 were outsourced, with half this new contingent of workers hired by the outsourced companies. The number of workers employed by VW rose from 300 to 500. Additionally, the plant began to design and produce a new cab and adopted the electronic engine, in compliance with legal requirements.

As a result, the profitability of the modular consortium drew the attention of the specialised press to its organisational concept. In the view of one of the managers of the company: 'The Resende operation is profitable, with low fixed costs, well able to handle market swings'. (*Diário do Vale Newspaper*, December 11, 2002). At the same time, this high productivity and profitability are used as benchmarks for the restructuring process that the company has been implementing since 2003 in other Brazilian plants. The trade union has warned that: '*In addition to this* [the lay-offs], *Volks wants to cut costs by 25% through implemented production processes such as the modular consortium, with mass outsourcing, among other measures*'. (SMABC – Sindicato dos Metalúrgicos do ABC. *Portal Sindical dos Metalúrgicos do ABC* website, May 4, 2006).

Labour Relations in the modular consortium

During this initial phase, the modular consortium project was particularly noteworthy for its innovations in the production organisation field, although the plant offered few innovations in terms of technology. Robots operate only in the paintwork section and in the welding booths, elsewhere manual labour prevails. In terms of labour relations, concerns have been fairly orthodox. Since the start-up of operations at this plant, Arbix and Zilbovicius (1997: 469) have already noted the lack of creative flair in the organisation of working groups or the establishment of group activities. Although the plant modules are organised on the basis of production cells and multi-tasking, there are no indications of any effective worker involvement – despite the Factory Committee and the Trade Union – in any processes that would endow the workers with more clout in the work-place (cf. Stewart *et al.*, 2005).

However, VW and its partners have deployed significant efforts to ensure that the new plant hires skilled and qualified employees who respond favourably to training and the new work arrangements. At the same time, it sought young workers with no earlier manufacturing experience (only 17 per cent came from the metallurgy sector) and with weak Trade Union experience[6] (cf. Ramalho and Santana, 2002), as highlighted by the words of the VW Human Resources Manager:

> The skilled worked who began here in 1996 had no bad habits. This is also a reality because the market was not an automotive market, the staff were developed within our business, and even the Trade Union did not have this experience from an automotive standpoint (...).
>
> The fact that we have no bad habits in the region, and that we developed the skilled worker in the work-place, as well as the fact that the Trade Union itself had no experience with the automotive sector, helped greatly.

It is easier to imprint a specific type of production-related behaviour on a work force with this profile. The quest for consensus solutions and a cooperative stance is fairly widely disseminated among all those working with the 'consortium'. At Resende, the need for co-operation is presented even more emphatically, as, in addition to the need for worker cooperation, the VW partner companies must also cooperate among themselves, prompting an ongoing negotiation process in many different sectors and at several levels. However, this commitment does not seem to appear in issues related to more democratic work force management.

In the management field, informal labour recruitment processes demonstrate a conservative management profile, imposing controls over the 'origins' of the workers. 'Personal indicators' from either modular consortium workers or managers are more important than the formal selection process established by VW and the other firms. This strategy is backed by direct links to workers through only a few corporate tiers, with the discourse of commitment to the company prompted by the need for cooperation. For the managers, cooperation among various levels and segments and reaching consensus solutions is a condition required for the existence of the modular consortium. Efforts to establish negotiating channels in order to reach such solutions is even expressed through the implementation of suggestion programmes or similar schemes that require worker participation, as noted by a Module administrator:

> Three times a week, I halt the plant for ten minutes, so that groups can gather together naturally in order to discuss the problems inherent to their area. This is an investment that I make in my work force. There is no one who knows the work better than they do. By making good use of this experience, we ensure that they chat for these ten minutes in the quest for excellence in quality and productivity, and even for upgrading their own working conditions.

Additionally, several programmes are run by the various modules that encourage worker participation in resolving technical production problems, where there is no interface with either the Trade Union or the Factory Committee. These programmes are the best way of ensuring worker compliance with production targets that are currently available to management, as work force remuneration policies are restricted – there are no extra payments beyond wages and the small percentage of the firm's profits that are negotiated annually by the trade union. However, there are modules with no mechanism for resolving problems or requesting worker participation in thinking about the production system, opting only for traditional relationships.

Consequently, traditional work force management practices continue, where the role of the supervisor is strengthened through leadership training sessions, with stand-alone strategies created in each model to respond to specific needs. This management profile may also be assessed through the characteristics of institutional performance appraisal tools, and the absence of more daring variable remuneration policies.

As benefits and incentives policies are widely used by modern enterprises to obtain cooperative conduct, in this context, we can add to management's brew, high regional unemployment rates, a work force with limited (and sometimes no) industrial experience, and a production segment based on a small number of workers (See *inter alia*, Durand and Stewart, 1998; Danford, 1999). These are all factors that allow the modular consortium to seek non-conflict mechanisms which lie outside the job itself.

Trade union activities

In Brazil's auto-assembly industry, negotiations between trade unions and management over wages and working conditions have passed through some important stages, during the late 1970s and early 1980s, when the trade union movement was restructured, to the point of being called the 'new trade unionism'. In fact, this special time began with strikes against multinational companies in the auto-assembly industry, establishing a generation of trade union members who were fairly critical of Brazil's corporatist trade union tradition. Trade unionism built up ample power through its mobilisations and became an important political player, not only in collective negotiations but also in discussions of labour laws and working conditions.

This scenario changed significantly with the deregulation of the Brazilian market during the 1990s. This new context brought in fresh investments, with competition and the quest for new productivity standards rapidly ushering in flexible production concepts. Despite their accumulated power, trade unions are currently finding it very hard to deal with new management strategies, particularly after the auto-assemblers moved to new regions far from the most active trade unions in the industrial belt around the City of São Paulo (cf. Stewart *et al.*, 2005).

The presence of an important auto-assembler like VW in Resende offered many challenges to the local Trade Union. In addition to having to negotiate with experienced managers, the Trade Union leaders had to restructure practices developed over decades of relationships with the steel sector, due to the presence of one of Brazil's leading steel complexes in neighbouring Volta Redonda, built during the 1940s.

> For those of us in the trade union, this was a new experience (…). We had a trade union policy that was closely linked to the CSN steel complex, which is a large enterprise. (…) We had this metalworker culture. (…) With the arrival of Volkswagen first (…) this was something quite new (…). Why? We did not know about

this (...) as the VW operating system is unique worldwide, it is modular. (...) There was this impact of using modules (...). So initially, we had a behavioural clash, in terms of the CSN steel complex. (...) Then we had another clash within Volkswagen itself, through the conduct of the modules that worked in different ways. Each had its own human resources policy. (President, Metalworkers' Trade Union, Volta Redonda, Rio de Janeiro, November 2001).

However, VW never attempted to conceal the fact that part of its plan for building its plant in this region was due to the establishment of labour relations differing from those found in more traditional industrial areas. On the other hand, the Metalworkers Trade Union saw the arrival of this venture as an opportunity to create more jobs in the region, with a 'flagship enterprise' within its field of operation. Rated by VW as more amendable to its corporate interest, the Trade Union immediately understood the meaning of signing up a new and different group of workers among its members.

Nevertheless, optimism generated by the possibility of new jobs may have given the false impression that the Trade Union would be neutralised particularly because it lacked experience for acting and negotiating in this industrial sector. Although Trade Union leaders were always guided by the spirit of reconciliation, during the early years of its operation, they soon perceived the difficulties encountered in dealing with the modular consortium, which also showed that the organisational strategy of this consortium to a certain extent weakened the companies in the face of any assertive expressions by the workers (cf. Ramalho and Santana, 2002). According to a Trade Union official at Resende in 1999:

the modular consortium is very vulnerable (...), because if you halt one sector, no matter how unimportant it may be, you halt the entire production line, you understand? We never discard the idea of a halt here... when dialog drags to a halt at the negotiating table, and no consensus is reached.

Despite its lack of experience, just a year after the plant came on-stream, the Trade Union called its first stoppage in November

1997. This was to be the first of a series of clashes that resulted in a one-week strike in August 1999. This strike was triggered by wage issues, which were among the comparative cost advantages justifying the establishment of this auto-assembler at Resende. The gap in wages was – and still is – significant, compared to those in other industrialised regions. Another result of the strike was the establishment of a Factory Committee, together with trade union action linked closely to factory-floor needs (cf. Ramalho and Santana, 2002).

> The strike was highly positive, [...]especially the formal acceptance of a factory committee by the company. Today we have a factory committee with job stability, democratically elected and with a better possibility of representing all shop floor workers. (Director of the Metalworkers' Trade Union, 1999).

An analysis of the Trade Union activities since 1996, when the company was inaugurated, shows that the Trade Union experience built up during its few years in operation has been following a learning curve in relation to this new situation. Not only has this entity adapted rapidly to the practices of the auto-assembly sector, but it has also attempted to join nationwide movements, like in 1999, when a national strike of workers in car factories was initiated at the VW plant in Resende.

After this decade in operation of the VW Plant at Resende, it appears that the local Trade Union, despite it defensive strategy, has shown a reasonable level of organisation. Over the past two years, the Trade Union has been undergoing an internal restructuring. In 2005, a workers group broke away from the *Força Sindical* entity of which it had been a member since 1992, whose trade union practices called for a partnership with the companies in order to generate jobs and maintain businesses in the region. With this Trade Union joining the Workers' Unified Confederation (*CUT*), political forces in this region were reshuffled, indicating the development of trade union practices that are not all that different from their predecessors, but with more democratisation of some decision-taking processes, resulting in more worker participation in decisions affecting their interests.[7]

What VW learned from these negotiations with its partners and the local Trade Union is that, in order to ensure a steady production flow at the plant, it must 'command' wage discussions on the factory floor. To do so, it stepped up its participation as the main negotiator for the entire 'consortium'. Furthermore, it had to accept the existence of a Factory Committee. Initially, according to the logic of the modular concept, VW formally refused to establish collective negotiating channels, as it had done at its plant in the ABC industrial belt around São Paulo, feeling that many of these arrangements were the tasks of individual members of the 'consortium'. However, this proved a source of problems, with informal discussions and negotiations taking place throughout the entire plant, until a proper Factory Committee was established.

The Factory Committee

The Factory Committee represents all workers of the modular consortium, and its directorate is elected in a secret ballot for a two year mandate. Any worker of the modular consortium can vote and be elected, but this does not extend to workers of the sub-contracted firms. At this moment, the Factory Committee has two members, one of them is the coordinator. Its action is regulated by an agreement between the firms of the modular consortium and the local metalworkers' trade union. While the Union deals with issues related to wages, the Committee is entitled to act and to interfere in conflicts on the shop floor. It is a quite contradictory political organisation since it defends workers against authoritarian behaviour by management and at the same time joins management for the improvement of productivity. There is also an intense dispute with the local trade union in terms of organisation inside the plant, since the Factory Committee is independent of the Union.

VW formally agreed to set up a Factory Committee in Resende and to institutionalise this type of worker organisation in a context that included the formal adherence to the Mercosur Southern Cone Common Market Agreement by the Volkswagen workers in 1999 (which stipulates that all VW plants in Latin America must have in-house employee representation). This was only part of a context however, which included the efforts of the local Trade Union and pressures from the World Workers Committee,[8] in addition to the one-week strike in the plant in 1999. This Committee is currently in its third term of office, and has played an important role in the quest to democratise labour relations on the factory floor, as well as extending the discussion lists submitted by the local Trade Union.

The Factory Committee is regulated by a Collective Agreement signed by the Trade Union and the firms of the modular consortium. This agreement demarcates the political field of activity of this Committee, preventing it from taking steps on issues related to juridical aspects; neither does it represent outsourced workers. Moreover, it is forbidden to undertake any politically-related activities in the factory, such as calling stoppages and meetings. However, these legal constraints do not prevent this Committee from involvement with workers employed by the outsourced companies, as well as calling brief stoppages and small meetings.

When analysing the political performance of the Factory Committee in its first two terms of office, the experience built up through representation-related activities resulted in a difference in quality in the political activities performed during these two periods. Actions shifted from a standpoint grounded mainly on management demands and the orders and influences of the Trade Union leader during the first term of office (1999–2002), to a more autonomous position in terms of the management and the Trade Union. Added to this there was an appreciable expansion of interventions in situations of conflict and resistance (stoppages and lightning meetings) during the second term of office (2002–2004) (Francisco, 2005).

More than six years after this Committee was established, the alterations in the factory, the Trade Union and the Committee itself require a fresh analysis of its political actions. As an example of these changes, on the one hand the significant expansion of production and the number of workers employed at the plant may be mentioned, and on the other the radical change in the relationship between the Committee and the Trade Union.

The changes in its relationship with the Trade Union took place from its third term of office onwards, which began in January 2005, due to sweeping political changes in the aegis of the Trade Union itself, already mentioned above, which forced it to build closer links with workers. The tighter links in these relationships are reflected in the participation of one of the members of the Factory Committee in the current Trade Union elections. On the other hand, the changes in the modular consortium required intensive actions by the Factory Committee, mainly with the additional shift. The significant increase in the number of outsourced workers also stepped up the demands made on the Committee, even though it was unable to respond to these demands from the outsourced workers, under the Collective Agreement.

Another important alteration behind the political actions of the Factory Committee took place through the organisations of the VW Corporation Factory Committees at the nationwide level, through the National Committee which was established in July 2005. This Committee organises 27,400 workers at five plants, and one of its purposes is to cluster worker rights and benefits together in a single collective convention. This organisation ensured closer contacts among VW Factory Committees in Brazil, offering hopes of exchanges of experiences among Committees located in very distant regions and linked to trade unions under different banners, in order to step up the bargaining power of the Factory Committees at the corporate level. Moreover, the political articulation between the Factory Committees and the Trade Unions, handled by the National Committee, may well prove fruitful for protecting worker interests at times of crisis.

The political activities of the Committee are handled on a daily basis by two members elected to represent the 'consortium' workers. At the external level, the Factory Committee is demonstrating an ability to interact with others. When attending seminars and workshops organised by the company – seeking the commitment of the Factory Committee and the Trade Union to maintaining the business – the Factory Committee wins in terms of its knowledge of the company and the corporation. This also means that it is gaining information regarding future investments and possibilities for expansion or shrinkage in employment. There are also situations where the Factory Committee could build up closer links with other management levels, which could be useful in negotiating situations.

Another aspect of the outside activities of the Factory Committee consists of its participation in the actions undertaken by other Factory Committees, as well as the National and World Committee and other Trade Union entities. If on the one hand this allows exchanges of experience and the build-up of knowledge in terms of political action, on the other it also allows the Resende Factory Committee to build up its own identity, based on its difference with its peers.

If the Committee can acquire knowledge and build up contacts with other representatives and institutions through its relationships outside the plant, building up more political experience, from the standpoint of trade union activities, it is in the daily routine of the plant that it gains expertise in playing the role of the worker representative. As there are few tiers in the modular consortium, with each module operating as a business unit with its own manager and some production supervisors, depending on the size of the module – individual issues are submitted by workers to their immediate supervisors. If no solution is reached, they are then forwarded to the Module Manager.

The way in which production is organised at this plant, in small enterprises, endows the work of the Factory Committee with a different dynamic, compared to other Volkswagen Committees in Brazil. These dynamics are also affected by working in cells and teams, as well as the participation and suggestions programmes, as many issues are settled at these levels, particularly those related to working conditions. Along these lines, it is not surprising that the Committee is contacted by a steady stream of workers from the outsourced companies, who are not covered by the mechanisms for settling problems used by the modules. In several situations, the Committee responds to complaints from the outsourced workers related to labour relations and working conditions. These actions are not publicised, but they do effectively occur during the daily work of the Factory Committee, constituting a universe of demands that range from workers whose work-books have not been signed through to high-risk situations or health hazards.

The manner in which this Committee operates within the modular consortium is being shaped by its daily routines, through situations that arise and the open conflicts that can flare up very rapidly, depending on the issues involved, while building up expertise in the field of political action. The surprise factor and the threat of adverse effects on production and productivity are the most effective tactics available to the Committee. However, there is a certain authoritarian tendency among the module management which contradicts the challenges of a more democratic manufacturing regime, and this strengthens the institutional fabric of the Factory Committee. This management profile is apparent in the constraints faced by the Trade Union and the Committee on issues related to production, such as work pace.

The purpose presented by the company for the existence of the Factory Committee is grounded, like all the others found in Volks- wagen Corporation, on building up a cooperative relationship with the workers, so that the company can avoid situations of conflicts with adverse effects on productivity and its market ranking. Due to the modular consortium profile, which means that Volkswagen must reach a consensus every day among its suppliers in terms of production targets and quality ratings, the Factory Committee is also faced by the need for political action ruled by this con- sensus. However, in contrast to other Volkswagen Plants, the members of the Resende Factory Committee have a task that is certainly more complex: building up relationships with eight differ- ent companies and management cultures, as well as their respective administrations.

Along these lines, the members of the Committee negotiate on a daily basis with various managers in several different companies, and when they adopt a face-off strategy, they must also organise workers in several different companies. Even though the workers are closely identified with Volkswagen and the modular consortium, they are hired, trained and supervised by various administrations that are shaped by different corporate cultures. Consequently, even though Volkswagen understands the role of the Factory Committee, for the modular consortium, the VW Human Resources Adminis- tration is under pressure from its partners to control its political activities. This is due to the fact that halting any segment of the production process means that the halt will be caused by workers employed by the partner companies, rather than Volkswagen workers.

As a result, the actions of the Factory Committee have a tightly demarcated scope, which does not include issues related to either production or labour relations. Consequently, this may disappoint those who assign it a role that it effectively does not play in its daily activities, such as representing workers in 'matters such as the pace of work, wage standards and relationships with the management' (Cardoso, 1997). In the consortium, only in terms of relationships with management does the Factory Committee demonstrate its clout. Wage standards still remain the prerogative of the Trade

Union, which does not even intervene in the pace of production, as this is the exclusive prerogative of Management.

An analysis of the political activities performed by the Factory Committee in the modular consortium in the course of its history is also vital. It shows how politically organised workers have been able to establish their own history through various experiences despite being shaped by the format of the organisation of production and the extra-political relationships that develop within this context. Along these lines, the political actions performed by the Committee are the outcome of the introduction of its members to this web of relationships over time. By opting for different strategies, aiming at either reconciliation or resistance, this embodies a political subject that is different from that imagined by the company and the Trade Union in late 1999. The various experiences built up over the years in different contextual situations open up possibilities for political actions that are shaped by the quest for consensus, appropriate to the modular consortium, but also through relationships of conflict arising from the protection of worker interests.

Conclusion

The experience of the modular consortium set up by VW at Resende has become a production process organisation model for the world's auto-assembly industry, creating standards and strategies that may be viewed as innovative in terms of inter-firm relationships and new processes intended to boost industrial productivity. However, in terms of the workers, these new management strategies, although insisting that changes could benefit workers at all levels of the organisation, still retain characteristics that are far from granting factory workers more power.

When discussing this issue, Stewart *et al.* (2005) affirm that lean production systems appear in a paradoxical relationship with trade unions, as the latter depend upon and at the same time attempt to challenge significant aspects of the given autonomy. This would be one of the core characteristics of the despotic hegemonic regime (Burawoy, 1985), which results in an increase in managerial control, a reduction in worker control over work, and an attack on trade union rights.

Within the context of plants working with flexibilised production, the possibility of political action handled through various types of worker organisations in the production sector, consisting of factory committees, councils or trade union delegates, is taking a new shape. The political activities undertaken by trade unions require other types of mediation and spokespersons to deal with management strategies that attempt to link worker subjectivity more strongly to production requirements.

The experience with flexible production within the context of a country such as Brazil raises important issues: Government policies for reproducing the work force were severely affected by neo-liberal type outreach policies, resulting in workers becoming more dependent on labour contracts, as their reproduction through public services became more difficult. In this context of widespread unemployment and restructured labour-saving plants, the agenda for trade union action was expanded beyond the factory and the manufacturing space where work was protected and had to be connected to other forms of political militancy. This explains the importance acquired by the various types of work-place organisation.

For the modular consortium, the possibility of undermining the political actions of the Factory Committee through the incessant quest for consensus solutions is limited by the concept of the more fragmented production organisation as well as the demands of lean production and the managerial diversity of the many partners. These elements endow the relationships between management and workers with a conservative approach, while strengthening the precarious nature of labour relations in the outsourced companies. Added to low automation and the consequent intensification of effort and working hours, these elements create an environment of conflict of interests where the Factory Committee and the Trade Union both acquire relevant roles in protecting worker interests. As a result, the Committee gains importance, together with the Trade Union, where the political aspects of its actions extend beyond the role that was initially conferred on it.

Consequently, the profile of the modular consortium constrains and shapes the political actions of worker organisations, but does not prevent the Factory Committee from building up its own identity. This is more visible as its political actions become clearer, presenting the factory floor as an arena of consensus and dissent, cooperation and conflict, tolerance and dispute. In other words, it reveals the factory as a political arena as well as a site of manufacturing innovation.

The track record of the modular consortium Factory Committee and the relationships that it has developed with its many different subjects (companies, workers, management and trade union) over time clearly indicate the alterations in its political action mechanisms and the representations built up by its members regarding its role in the regulation of production and the employment relationship. In sum, the case of VW in Resende shows that despite the implementation of the 'modular system', with strategies of fragmenting and weakening worker participation, after ten years of existence, it has also created conditions for new forms of worker resistance. Moreover, although under great pressure from management, workers' organisations in the factory, such as the Factory Committee and trade union, have learned new ways of defending labour rights in this new context, and have moved closer to the needs of workers on the shop floor.

Notes

1 The data, information and interviews supporting the text are the partial findings of research projects backed by CNPQ and FAPERJ (Programa Cientistas do Nosso Estado) in Brazil, institutions to which we are grateful.
2 Factory Committee is the name given by workers to what VW calls the 'Employee's Internal Representation'. It was established through an agreement between the company and the local trade union. It is composed of two representatives, elected directly by workers of the 'modular consortium', with a two year mandate. It is also similar to what in some countries is referred to as Works Council.
3 The *Novo Regime Automotivo* intended to consolidate and attract investments to the auto-assembly sector. Its main objectives were: (1) to keep the main auto-assemblers and auto components industries in operation, already established in Brazil; (2) to structure Brazilian enterprises in this sector; (3) to attract new companies and encourage the construction of new plants; (4) to consolidate the Mercosul Southern Cone Common Market and strengthen the position of Brazil as its main player.
4 CIPA is an organised group that exists inside every plant. It is composed in equal terms by representatives of employees and employers with the specific task of preventing accidents on the shop floor. The CIPA is regulated by Brazilian Labour Laws and it is compulsory. The workers' representatives at CIPA have job security during the period of their mandate.

5   Other than workers in food companies, asset security, transport and civil construction.

6   In Brazil, trade unions represent all workers in a given geographical area, both affiliated and unaffiliated and there can only be one union for each category of workers. Workers of the 'modular consortium' are linked to the Metalworkers' Trade Union of the South of Rio de Janeiro State, which is responsible for negotiating wages, working conditions and making collective agreements with all companies of this trade in the region.

7   For example, instead of decisions related to the 'Participation on Profits and Results' (PLR) (which is part of the workers' remuneration package) being negotiated only by management and trade union officials, for the first time in the history of the 'modular consortium', they were taken in an open assembly with shop-floor workers inside the plant.

8   At VW, the Factory Committees are part of the history of the corporation in Brazil since the 1980s, with the organisation of its workers at the worldwide level dating back to the 1970s; in 1999, the World Worker Committee was formally established.

References

Abreu, A., Gitahy, L., Ramalho, J.R., and Ruas, R. (1999) 'Industrial Restructuring and Inter-Firm Relations in the Auto-Parts Industry in Brazil', *Occasional Papers 20*. Institute of Latin American Studies, University of London.

Abreu, A., Beynon, H., Ramalho, J.R. (2000) 'The Dream factory – VW's modular production system in Resende, Brazil', *Work, Employment and Society*, vol. 14, no. 2, Cambridge, UK, June 2000.

Arbix, G. (2000) 'Guerra Fiscal e Competiçã Intermunicipal por Novos Investimentos no Setor Automotive Brasileiro'. Dados, vol. 43, no. 1. Rio de Janeiro, IUPERJ, pp. 5–43.

Arbix, G. and Zilbovicius, M. (1997) 'O Consórcio Modular da VW: um novo modelo de produção'. *De JK a FHC – A Reinvenção dos Carros*, Arbix, G. & Zilbovicius, M. (eds). São Paulo, Scritta.

Arbix, G. and Rodrígues-Pose, Andrés (1999) 'Estratégias de Desperdício – A Guerra entre Estados e Municipios por Novos Investimentos e as Incertezas do Desenvolvimento? Novos Estudos *CEBRAP*, no. 54. São Paulo, Cebrap.

Burawoy, M. (1985) *The politics of production*. London: Verso.

Cardoso, A.M. (1997) 'O sindicalismo corporativo não é mais o mesmo', *Novos Estudos CEBRAP*. São Paulo, CEBRAP. pp. 97–119.

Diário do Vale Newspaper. (Various issues). www.diariodovale.com.br

Danford, A. (1999) *Japanese Managemnet Techniques and British Workers*. London: Mansell.

Durand, J.P. and Stewart, P. (1998) 'Manufacturing Dissent? Burawoy in a Franco-Japanese Workshop', *Work, Employment and Society*, vol. 12, no. 1, March. pp. 145–59.

Francisco, Elaine Marlova V. (2005) *A Comissão Enxuta: ação política na fábrica do consórcio modular em Resende*. São Paulo, EDUSC/ANPOCS.

Gazeta Mercantil Newspaper, Rio de Janeiro, April 9, 2001, p. 1-b.

Ramalho, José Ricardo and Santana, Marco A. (2002) *Um perfil dos metalúrgicos da Volkswagen de Resende-RJ*, Rio de Janeiro, Unitrabalho/UFRJ. Relatório Final de Pesquisa.

SMABC – Sindicato dos Metalúrgicos do ABC. *Portal Sindical dos Metalúrgicos do ABC*. www.smabc.org.br

Stewart, P., Ramalho, José R., Danford, A.; Pulignano, V. and Santana, M.A. (2005) 'Novas estratégias gerenciais e a qualidade de vida no trabalho na indústria automobilística (Grã-Bretanha, Brasil e Itália)'. In *Revista Latinoamericana de Estudios del Trabajo*, 10, N. 17, 2005. Montevideo, ALAST. pp. 165–94.

7
The Quest for Flexibility in the Mexican Auto Parts Industry: Three Tales from a Multinational Company

Christian Lévesque[1]

In the search to achieve higher levels of flexibility, employers are using various means, such as coercive comparisons and threats of relocation, to increase management discretion and transform the terms and conditions of employment. This management strategy of continuous change poses a challenge to traditional forms of work regulation and has generated tensions and conflict.

In Mexico, these attempts to make workplace rules more flexible do not seem to have generated the same kind of union opposition as in Canada or the U.S. (de la Garza, 1998; Pries, Garcia and Gutierrez, 2000). A tradition of strong state intervention in labour relations and the historic alliance between official unions and the governing party (the PRI) appear to limit the ability of local unions to oppose the allegedly market-driven changes to workplace rules (Dombois, 1999). Moreover, despite the weakening of the historic alliance between the PRI and the CTM (Confederación de Trabajadores de México, the Mexican trade union confederation), official unions in Mexico continue to espouse the competitiveness strategies promoted by both employers and the state (Bensusán, 2006). Indeed, the CTM and COPARMEX, the Mexican employers' confederation, are promoting a new work culture characterised by workplace flexibility and a community of interests between workers and employers. According to Bensusán (2000), the Mexican industrial relations model has evolved from authoritarian corporatism, in which workplace behaviour was dictated from on high, towards micro-corporatism, in which the official unions, in return for the recognition of their presence in the new factories, accept the competitive logic of their export-oriented employers.

The combination of accelerated workplace change and significant changes in the political economy of workplace power relations has prompted observers to argue that trade unions have little choice but to acquiesce in this overriding quest to increase flexibility (de la Garza, 2003). Local managers would also appear to be caught in this spiral. They cannot escape the pressure exerted by multinational corporations (MNCs) on their subsidiaries and suppliers to increase work and employment flexibility. Thus by appointing internal managers, developing corporate culture and making coercive comparisons, MNCs are said to be ensuring that common practices and understandings of competitive performance are being diffused. Local managers, it is argued, have to internalise these practices and, like local unions, have no choice but to accept the requirements of the new flexible workplaces.

It is our contention that such a scenario underestimates the capacity of local actors to cope with institutional and market constraints. We argue that workplace regimes have a relative autonomy and that local actors can strategise even in a context in which they are tightly constrained by institutional and corporate policies. The theoretical challenge is then to ascertain how local actors are coping with the pressure to increase flexibility. Are they internalising the requirements of the new flexible workplaces, adapting it to their own local environments or developing their own approaches? Are managers and union representatives cooperating with each other, opposing each other or working in parallel? This article addresses these questions through an analysis of three case studies conducted within the same MNC operating in the Mexican auto parts industry. Over the period of the study, this multi-division MNC shifted from a decentralised to a centralised approach based on a unilateral model of workplace flexibility.

The first part of this chapter examines the evolution of the economic and institutional arrangements in the Mexican automotive industry. We then give an overview of the study before detailing the results of our case studies, which highlight three distinct paths towards flexibility. In conclusion, we examine the salient features of our findings regarding the emerging patterns of flexibility and workplace relations against a background of increasing regional integration.

Economic and institutional changes in the Mexican automotive industry

In recent decades, the Mexican automobile industry has gradually entered the global economy and become a major player in the North American auto industry. The number of vehicles produced in Mexico tripled between 1985 and 2002, when approximately 1.3 million passenger cars were produced (Carrillo, 2004:11). In the early 1970s, the industry's output was destined solely for the domestic market; today, more than 70 per cent of vehicles produced are exported (Carrillo, 2004). A large part of these exported vehicles are produced for the U.S. and the Canadian markets. This regional integration has been combined with a spatial reorganisation of production. In the 1980s and early 1990s, new factories were constructed in the centre and north of the country (Ford Hermosillo, GM Ramos Arizpe and GM Silao, Nissan Aguascalientes) (Arteaga, 2000). The establishment of NAFTA (North American Free Trade Agreement), which requires cars to have a high North American content, has forced U.S., Asian and European auto parts suppliers to set up plants in Mexico (Gereffi, 2003). According to Carrillo, in 2000 there were 875 auto parts companies, of which 34 per cent were subsidiaries of foreign companies (Carrillo, 2004:115).

This rapid integration of the automotive industry into the North American economy has prompted domestic and foreign employers to reduce production costs and to increase flexibility. Over the last decade, in spite of a continuous growth in productivity, workers have lost half of their purchasing power (Servin, 2002). The decline in real wages cannot be dissociated from the growth of employment in the 'maquilladoras', where unions are virtually non-existent and pay is lower than in the more traditional auto part plants (de la O Martínez, 2001; Carrillo and Partida, 2004). This downward trend is also closely linked to the evolution of the labour market. The formal labour market is unable to absorb the strong demographic growth that characterises Mexico's young workforce. As a result, a high proportion of young labour market entrants must seek work in the informal economy, where roughly 50 per cent of the population works (Salas and Zepeda, 2003: 525).[2]

The requirements of regional integration are also giving rise to significant changes in the content of collective agreements. Over the last decade, both functional flexibility, which is achieved by reorganising work, notably through job rotation, task redefinition and the creation of teams, and numerical flexibility, which is achieved through the use of temporary or contract labour, outsourcing and off-shoring, have increased considerably (Carrillo, 2004; de la Garza, 1998; Dombois, 1999; Montiel Hernández, 2003; Pries *et al.*, 2000; Tuman, 2003). Seniority rights are gradually being eliminated and replaced by such criteria as disciplinary record and workers' competences or skills, all of which increase management discretion.

Despite the regional integration of the automotive industry, the institutional regime has been quite resilient. In fact, many of the authoritarian elements of the regime have remained intact and some have been reinforced rather than undermined (Middlebrook and Zepeda, 2003). The changing geometry of party political power in Mexico, which culminated in the election of Vicente Fox in 2000, has not fundamentally altered either the rules of the game or the principles governing union and management action (Bensusán, 2006; Bensusán and Cook, 2003).[3] Government officials have not dismantled the complex arrangement of legal and administrative controls regulating wages, contract negotiations, strikes and union registration.

Official unions continue to play an important role within the state administration in return for their cooperation in industrial and political matters. This is particularly the case with regard to labour courts, which have significant decision-making power in areas such as the determination of union representativeness, union registration and the legality of strikes (Bensusán, 2006). Official unions, notably the CTM, also support the government economic strategy, which relies on low wages and flexible workplaces as a basis for international comparative advantage (Middlebrook and Zepeda, 2003). The CTM actively promotes this strategy and condemns any actions from its affiliates that could undermine it. Conversely, the CTM, which is the largest union in the automotive industry, does not support initiatives launched by either workplace or industrial unions to establish coordinated negotiations. The result has been a decentralised process of plant-by-plant negotiation with no formal centralised coordination (Huxley, 2003).

At the workplace level, several studies undertaken over the last decade show that local unions in the automotive industry, notably those affiliated to the CTM, have adopted a passive attitude and been completely excluded from the implementation of workplace change (Arteaga, 2000; Bayón, 1997; de la Garza, 2003; Tuman, 2003). In the global arena, Mexico would seem to be fertile ground for MNCs seeking to establish flexible workplaces. Thus the integration of the North American automotive industry, combined with institutional robustness, appears to limit the capacity of local actors to oppose the drive towards greater numerical and functional flexibility.

An alternative hypothesis – the core focus of this chapter – suggests that local actors, irrespective of transnational pressures and institutional setting, have a relative autonomy. Our primary focus in this article concerns the relative importance of union capabilities or what we label power resources to shape patterns of workplace flexibility. The analysis of power in the workplace presents daunting methodological challenges because of the need to unravel the different dimensions of power relationships between actors: structural (as in the wage relationship and the place of actors in the overall institutional framework), relational (as in the resources that actors can mobilise in particular circumstances) and contextual (or opportunity structures, as in the particular sets of circumstances in which the relations between actors take place). Drawing on pre-vious analyses of variations in union capacity (Dufour and Hege, 2002; Frost, 2001; Lévesque and Murray, 2002, 2005, Pries *et al.*, 2000), three power resources appear to be of particular importance for local unions faced with workplace change: *internal solidarity,* which relates to the mechanisms developed in the workplace to ensure democracy and collective cohesion among workers; *external solidarity,* which refers to the capacity of local unions to work with their communities and to build horizontal and vertical coordination with other unions as well as the building of alliances among unions, community groups and social movements; and *strategic capacity* which refers to the discursive ability of local unions to shape and put forward their own agenda.

The question that remains to be answered is whether institutional and market constraints determine the pattern of flexibility at the local level or whether local actor capabilities to mobilise their power resources are still relevant.

Research method

This chapter reports findings from a study conducted between 1999 and 2005 in three plants operating in the automotive industry. These three plants are part of a division of a large conglomerate owned by Mexican and foreign capital. This conglomerate is active in the auto parts industry as well as in the telecommunications, aluminium and hospitality sectors. One key condition for open access to theses plants was the promise to protect their identities when reporting the data.

The local union in each of these plants is affiliated to the CTM, albeit in different ways. One of them is a 'sindicato de empresa' that is affiliated to the CTM at regional level but has no links with any industrial union. It manages its own union dues and hires specialist staff when needed. Accordingly, it enjoys considerable autonomy in the administration of union affairs. The other two workplace unions are branches of an amalgamated union that is part of the CTM, the *Sindicato de industria de la metal, mecanica, similares y connexos* (SITIMM). The SITIMM has 30 workplace branches and nearly 16,000 members. These branches are located in the state of Guanajuato in the centre of the country and are mainly in the automotive and metalworking industries. Contrary to established practice in many amalgamated CTM unions, these branches have elected executives and manage 75 per cent of the dues they collect.[4] The amalgamated union provides assistance to the branches during the biennial negotiations on the collective agreement.[5]

The data were collected in 1999, 2001, 2004 and 2005. Plant documents and collective agreements were analysed in order to ascertain the extent and scope of flexibility. At each site, interviews were conducted with plant managers, human resource and production managers, shop-floor representatives and members of the executive committee of the local union. The interviews were recorded in their entirety and transcribed to facilitate analysis. These semi-structured interviews covered a wide range of issues: the characteristics of the plants and the firm; plant history, structure and the type of relations established with the headquarter; the evolution of HR practices and work organisation; the evolution of flexible and numerical flexibility; history and evolution of union-management relations; union history, structure and internal dynamics; membership characteristics; the type of relations established with different external groups; and the nature and intensity of networks developed.

Our major hypothesis is that union power resources shape patterns of workplace flexibility. Union power resources cover three dimensions: internal solidarity, external solidarity and strategic capacity. *Internal solidarity* is measured by both objective indicators, such as the presence of a network of shop-floor representatives and paid-release time for union activities and mixed indicators such as the perceptions of worker solidarity (workers' participation in union meetings, workers' support of the union, etc.) and worker cohesion (notably, perceptions of workers' capacity to formulate demands and use pressure tactics). *External solidarity* is measured by the extent of workplace union participation in the larger union structure and the frequency of exchange with other workplace unions and with other groups in local communities. *Strategic capacity* is measured through union positions on workplace change and particularly flexibility initiatives. This third dimension of union power seeks to differentiate local unions according to their discursive capacity to adopt a strategy on workplace change that is different from that put forward by local management.

Patterns of flexibility and workplace relations

The multi-division MNC under scrutiny went through several changes over the period of the study. Until 2003, the national head office of the auto parts division allowed local managers considerable leeway in the management of HR and employment relations issues. Local managers had autonomy within the guidelines laid down by the division. In order to foster the adoption of best practices, head office set benchmarks and instituted an awards scheme for the plants obtaining the best results.

In 2003, the company adopted a more centralised approach. The HR department in each plant was dramatically downsized and the remaining personnel had to implement decisions taken at division headquarters. In particular, headquarters was seeking to increase flexibility by putting in place a unilateral model in which workers and the union were excluded from the decision-making process. Management expected unions and workers to follow the new 'best practices' model in order to restore the division's profitability.

It must be acknowledged that the profitability of the auto parts division has been declining since 2001 and hundreds of workers have been laid off, while some plants have simply been closed down.

The shift from a decentralised to a centralised approach has met with different kinds of responses from local managers. They range from compliance to open hostility and opposition. Union response has also been quite variable. As will become evident in this section, the response of local actors to the new top-down approach initiated by division headquarters has been quite variable in each of the three plants under study. Three distinct patterns of flexibility and workplace relations can be identified: full flexibility achieved by excluding the union, numerical flexibility attained through micro-corporatism and functional flexibility obtained through a contested joint regulation process.

Flexibility through union exclusion

The plant in question produces axles for small and medium-sized cars. It is highly integrated into the North-American industry and exports approximately 80 per cent of its output. It is located in an industrial town north of Mexico City. The facilities (cafeteria, showers, etc.) are very modern and the factory is surrounded by two brand new football fields for the exclusive use of plant employees. Over the period of the study, the workforce was quite stable with roughly 700 employees, of whom 500 are unionised.

Over the years, the plant has won several prizes and recognition from customers and divisional headquarters. At some point in 2000, it was regarded as the benchmark plant among the division's auto parts plants. Several changes were introduced over the period of our study, including cellular manufacturing, quality improvement groups and multi-skilling. Of the three plants in our study, it is the most advanced in terms of functional flexibility. Production is organised around cellular manufacturing, with each worker being responsible for operating three to four machines. In 2001, management introduced a scheme whose aim was to transfer as many maintenance tasks as possible to production workers. In each production cell, workers are now responsible for cleaning and repairing the machinery. Their work is supported and supervised by a maintenance worker, who also has the task of training the production workers. The introduction of this scheme created some tensions between production and maintenance workers, but management has been able to overcome these tensions and push on with the scheme.

Until 2003, workers were also involved in continuous improvement groups. These groups were considered by local managers as a key mechanism for identifying production and quality problems and for encouraging the workforce to cohere around a common corporate culture. In 2003, these groups were dissolved. Management had come to the conclusion that they were time consuming and did not deliver in terms of productivity increases and quality improvements. This decision did not prompt any reaction on the part of the union, as with many decisions taken by local managers. In fact, management has considerable freedom to introduce changes in work organisation and production. Managers make decisions on the content and implementation of change without any input from the union. The collective agreement does not limit the employer's freedom in this regard. He can change the organisation of work and transfer employees in accordance with operational requirements. The agreement places no restrictions either on the employer's freedom to outsource work or hire temporary workers, although neither option is extensively used.

HR practices are also designed to increase management control over the workers. The new practices are intended to strengthen both the collective and individual dimensions of the employment relationship. On the one hand, pays varies according to the skills of each individual employee, promotions and employee transfers are made on the basis of skills and employee benefits, in particular the length of annual leave and the bonus tied to it, fluctuate according to the employee's disciplinary record. Each worker's skills and abilities are posted up on large boards for everyone to see. On the other hand, managers and workers wear the same uniform and use the same cafeteria. Everything has been done to reduce the barriers between management and workers and to reinforce the idea that they form a team. Thus, within this collective entity, workers can distinguish themselves and emphasise their individuality. In other words, management and workers make up one big family, but within this family workers can be in competition with each other. The union is thus faced with an employer that is striving to introduce HR practices that clash directly with one of the main driving forces behind union action, namely the collective identity of workers.

Management has also adopted a discourse that fosters a community of interest with the union. Drawing on a unitarist vision of the firm's operations, management recognises the union's interests only to the extent that they coincide with its own. The plant's competitiveness determines all other goals. Any union demands not consistent with management objectives are deemed to be illegitimate. Nor does the employer recognise any autonomous activities the workplace union might engage in; they are seen at best as useless and at worst as counterproductive. At the local level, management deals only with the general secretary, thereby marginalising the other executive committee members and creating tensions within the union executive committee. By isolating the general secretary management is striving to achieve greater control over union actions. The success of this strategy can be illustrated by the extreme example of union training being provided by a consultant chosen and paid for by management.

These relations between management and union have developed in a context in which the union has few sources of power. It is relatively isolated: it has no links with other local unions in its industry or region and its participation in union activities tends to be confined to a single person. This isolation is combined with a lack of any mechanism to foster internal solidarity. More precisely, this union has not developed basic organisational mechanisms to promote internal solidarity and democracy. Shop-floor union representatives are virtually non-existent, even though plant size would seem to make them necessary, and paid release time for union officials is limited. The local union does not have an office inside the factory. The absence of such resources reduces the local union's capacity to communicate with its members. To put it bluntly, communication networks inside the union are elementary at best. To add to this rather gloomy portrait, it should be stressed that the legitimacy of union representatives appears to be precarious. The union executive changes every election, that is, after a three-year mandate. Thus, it is the union staffer who provides continuity in labour relations, which reduces the credibility of the local representatives among workers and management.

The weakening of the amalgamated industrial union which, following internal rivalries within the CTM, lost its right to represent workers at a large strategic plant to a more compliant amalgamated union, has led to union elections being much more vigorously contested. In the last election in 2005, there were seven candidates. The new general secretary, who had no prior union experience, won by one vote, with support from less than 20 per cent of the electoral base. The divisions within the union, combined with the workers' disaffection, have created an opportunity for management to seek to eliminate the local union. The outcome of management initiatives remains uncertain, but they will undoubtedly further undermine the legitimacy of the local union and give even greater discretion to management to pursue its flexibility objectives. Thus the social dynamics within the plant have enabled local managers to implement the unilateral approach put forward by divisional head office to enhance flexibility without any interference from the local union.

Flexibility through micro-corporatism

This plant assembles bodies for pick-up trucks. Workers are spread across three departments: the stamping, welding and painting departments. In 2002, the plant lost major contracts and the workforce gradually dropped from 1,000 unionised workers in 1999 to 200 in 2003. In 2005, employment started to climb again when the plant obtained a new contract.

During this period (1999–2005), there was no significant change in the organisation of work. The driving force behind work organisation is teamwork. Apart from the team leaders, who are unionised employees, the workers have few responsibilities. Team leaders are given a series of responsibilities that were previously entrusted to the first-line supervisors: allocation of tasks to team members, distribution of information, handling of complaints, etc. Even though rotation within teams is the exception rather than the rule, management has the leeway to transfer workers when there are bottlenecks in the production process. The only restriction on the movement of workers across teams and departments is an obligation on the employer to inform the union representatives twenty-four hours in advance. This constraint is more formal than real.

There have not been many changes in HR practices either. Management still favours an approach that emphasises both individualised practices, such as skills-based remuneration and individualised training plans, and collective practices (shared cafeteria, teamwork, etc.). That said, management does not enjoy the same degree of freedom as in the previous case. It can hire temporary workers only under specific circumstances and has to take into consideration workers' seniority when deciding on lay-offs and promotions.

Prior to 2003, management was not attempting to impose a unitarist vision of the plant's operation. It recognised that its interests did not always coincide with those of the workers, hence the potential for disagreements between management and the union. Nor was management seeking to assimilate the union or systematically reduce the scope of its actions. Rather than denying that conflicts exist, it favoured the creation of conflict-resolution mechanisms. Thus it advocated a pluralist vision of labour-management relations. The union's role in this approach was clearly defined. It was consulted prior to the introduction of workplace changes but it was management that made the decisions. In other words, union representatives were not bound by the decision and could disagree with management strategy. This consultative role enabled the union to get information and even influence management's initial stance, while at the same time maintaining its independence from management.

This pattern of union involvement developed in a context in which the union was not powerless. On the one hand, the union is not isolated. Union representatives participate in activities organised by the regional and industry unions, even though these external links rarely extend beyond the boundaries of the amalgamated union to which the local union is affiliated. On the other hand, the union has also developed its own internal resources: typically, an office in the factory, union paid release time and a shop steward system. However, in the context of a shrinking workforce, this system has been reduced to the minimum.

However, two significant changes did become evident following the 2003 lay-off, the first affecting union-management relations and the second the management of the internal labour market. Following the wave of lay-offs, which even included the HR manager, employment relations issues were taken up by the plant manager. He did not have much experience in this area and could not rely on the experience of other managers in the plant. In fact, the only person with expertise in industrial relations was the general secretary of the union, who has been in office for nearly twenty years. He is released full-time to engage in union activities and, over the years, has developed very close ties with management and has the plant manager's confidence.

To some extent, the general secretary became the functional equivalent of an HR manager. Accordingly, the plant manager not only consulted him but actively promoted his involvement in the decision-making process. As a result, the union found itself bound by management decisions and had to recommend the proposed changes to its members. To some extent, it is difficult under such circumstances to distinguish the union representative from management, so completely has he internalised the management discourse on the need for competitiveness in the global era. The union thus acts as a conveyor belt seeking to convince the workforce that changes are necessary and will have a positive impact on their factory's competitive position. In other words, the union has also espoused a unitarist vision that promotes the common interests of both workers and management.

The second major change concerns the management of the internal labour market. While seniority rights had always been predominant, during the lay-off workers' disciplinary records were also taken into account and played a significant part in the decision-making. They were also of primary importance when workers previously laid off were being recalled. The union was directly involved in the re-hiring of the laid-off workers. It could be argued that this is nothing new in Mexico, since unions have been involved in the hiring process through the use of the exclusion clause. What is genuinely new, however, is that workers are no longer being hired on the basis of their political or union allegiance; the crucial factor is whether or not they endorse the new work culture that fosters co-operation and a supposed community of interest between workers and employer. Greater use is also being made of temporary contracts in order to select workers who support this new work culture.

In short, with the cooperation of the union representative, management has significantly increased its internal and external flexibility. In doing so, the local actors did not follow the unilateral approach favoured by the divisional head office but they achieved the same results. The union general secretary internalised the new requirements of the flexible workplace to such an extent that union and management were able to develop a competitive alliance to safeguard workers' job. The general secretary was a key actor in the change process, but his close involvement in the decision-making process also generates a certain degree of scepticism among the workers. Both management and the general secretary recognise that they are treading a fine line.

Flexibility through contested joint regulation

This plant, located in a large industrial city north of Mexico, assembles car transmissions, mainly for export. In the early 1980s, it employed close to 5,000 workers. Since then, the number of workers has declined to 2,100, of whom 1,300 are unionised. Until 2003 this plant was the most advanced in terms of union involvement in the change process.

The local union was directly involved in decisions regarding the introduction of continuous improvement groups, an integrated quality management system and cellular manufacturing. Following the introduction of cellular manufacturing, the union negotiated a wage increase of 20 per cent. The union was also able to introduce specific mechanisms and measures to soften the effects of changes on the workers. For example, new jobs were evaluated jointly and a joint committee deals with potential complaints regarding transfers and promotions. Despite the existence of cellular manufacturing and skills-based pay, seniority continues to play an important role in both the deployment of workers and the determination of employee benefits. In short, in this plant, the union was able to obtain guarantees and protections following the introduction of functional flexibility. Management's ability to use temporary workers was also limited by the incorporation into the collective agreement of a clause stipulating a certain ratio of casual to permanent employees.

Two interrelated factors have helped to shape management-union relations in this plant. First, despite having established sophisticated human resources management programmes, management is not attempting either to assimilate the union or to impose a unitarist vision. Rather, it is putting forward a pluralist vision of the enterprise that encourages both parties to articulate problems and resolve disputes. Second, management is dealing with a local union that is able to draw on several sources of power. In addition to the presence of organisational mechanisms that help to ensure internal solidarity (a local union office in the plant, paid release time for union officials and a shop steward system), it tends to use more sophisticated communications mechanisms and has paid release time for shop stewards involved in resolving workers' problems. The local union is also well integrated into networks outside the plant. It has established regular relations with other local unions in the community and it participates in an information-sharing network on working conditions in the automotive industry.

The custom and practices established in this plant over more than a decade run counter to the unilateral model favoured by the national division head office. This model was received by both local management and union representatives with scepticism and incredulity. They had a different concept of what constituted 'best practices' for their plant. They formed an alliance to resist the new model and to demonstrate the effectiveness of the system of joint regulation they had forged over the years. Head office did not accept their arguments and the plant manager and the HR director were soon dismissed and replaced by a new team of managers. This radical action was followed by a series of moves designed to discredit the members of the union executive committee. This tactic was quite effective and created turmoil in the union. The union leaders faced a number of challengers in the 2004 election and all of them were voted out of office except for the general secretary.

It was against this background that the renegotiation of the collective agreement began. The new management team was striving not only to increase flexibility and reduce costs but also to undermine the local union's legitimacy once and for all. Two factors prevented management from achieving its goal. First, the new management team misread the dynamic within the local union. Management believed that the election reflected workers' dissatisfaction with trade unionism and collective representation. In fact, the election reflected their dissatisfaction with the old local leadership. This being so, the election results created an opportunity for young activists to take on new responsibilities and breathe new life into the union. The union was able to draw on this new generation of activists built up over the years through the shop steward structure. This dense network was an important source of power and renewal for the local union.

Second, the new management team also underestimated the capacity of the local union to tap into vertical and horizontal networks and structures in order to frame the narrative of the conflict. The local union used these networks during the negotiation to diffuse information and convince strategic actors that management's position and its demands were counter-productive and unreasonable. The union was able to counter management's discourse on the requirements of the new economy and the illegitimacy of the local union position. As well as reinforcing its position inside and outside the plant, it also prevented the state official from intervening in favour of management during the negotiation process.

Ultimately, management suffered an important set back and did not achieve its objective either in terms of flexibility enhancement or cost reduction. Perhaps most importantly, management was not able to win its power struggle with the union. In fact, a few months after the collective negotiations, a new management team tried to open up channels of communication with the local union in order to restore some form of joint regulation.

Conclusion

In our view, the Mexican case is an exemplary one for examining how actors cope with the requirements of the new economy. The rapid integration of the automotive industry into the regional economy, coupled with the fragile but still robust corporatist regime, seems substantially to reduce local actors' ability to cope with the pressure to increase flexibility.

Many unions face a difficult choice: either they accept the employer's competitive logic and engage in micro-corporatism or they are excluded from the decision-making process (Bayón, 1997; Arteaga, 2000). Local managers are also forced to increase workplace flexibility. In fact, both local union representatives and local managers seem to be locked into an iron cage with no room for manoeuvre. Nevertheless, our findings show that workplace relations are characterised by a certain degree of autonomy, that there is space for actors to shape workplace relations and patterns of flexibility. Our findings certainly point in this direction.

This study does not support the conventional top-down view, in which MNCs are portrayed as highly centralised organisations, coordinated by powerful headquarters that control the behaviour of local actors. Following a growing body of research (Almond *et al.*, 2006; Bélanger *et al.*, 2003; Bélanger and Edwards, 2006; Kristensen and Zeitlin, 2005; Martin and Beaumont, 1999; Pulignano, 2006), our results show that local managers use their resources and capabilities to put forward their own views on the firm's objectives and operations.

These views may be consistent with, complementary to or in opposition to other views within the MNC, notably those originating from head office. In one of our cases, where flexibility was achieved by excluding the union, the local managers' views were quite consistent with the model proposed by head office. In fact, the head office approach legitimised a more aggressive stance towards the local union. In the case of micro-corporatism, the plant manager opposed the unilateral model and union involvement was significantly increased. The plant manager used the union general secretary as the functional equivalent of a HR director. He was able to draw on his tacit knowledge in order to implement changes in the workplace. In the case of joint regulation, there was a clash between two concepts of 'best practice'. The plant and HR managers tried to build an alliance with the local union in order to resist the new top-down approach being promoted by head office. This strategy provoked intense conflict between the different layers of management and isolated the local managers. The absence of allies outside the plant put the local managers in a precarious position, which ultimately led to their dismissal.

Thus local managers are not passive agents who merely implement the policies laid down by headquarters. They shape the outcome of these policies and formulate strategies on the basis of their own views of how best to achieve the firm's objectives. They internalise the requirements of the new flexible workplaces but adapt them to their own local environment.

Our findings do not suggest either that local unions have no choice but to adapt passively to the drive to increase flexibility. Local union representatives can also alter and influence the patterns of flexibility. In order to do so, however, they must develop their power resources. In workplaces in which the local union is unable to mobilise its potential external and internal resources, it is by and large simply excluded from the change process. It does not appear to be a credible interlocutor for managers. Conversely, in workplaces in which local unions are able to mobilise their power resources, they tend to play a more active role in the change process, albeit in different ways. The local union in the micro-corporatism pattern is clearly locked into management decisions and has to endorse the firm's definition of its competitive requirements. In contrast, the local union in the contested joint regulation pattern enjoys a certain room for manoeuvre in order to develop its own agenda and to undertake independent action. Drawing on its internal and external resources, the union was able to strategise and put forward its own vision of the firms' operations as well as of the emerging conflict with management. The local union's capacity to frame the narrative of the conflict proved to be an invaluable resource and prevented external actors from intervening in the conflict. In the end, the local union was able to prevent management from achieving its goal of increasing flexibility by imposing a unilateral model.

Overall, this study shows that, even in a context in which institutional and corporate policies are placing strong constraints on local actors, workplace regimes have a relative autonomy and local actors can devise strategies that enable them to be involved in shaping those regimes. The implementation of flexibility through the imposition of a unilateral model is based on the assumption that such a model is more efficient, irrespective of institutional and local arrangements. In two of our cases, this assumption was challenged and alternative models prevailed. In a context in which there are competing narratives about the efficiency of workplace regimes, local actors, particularly local unions, must develop their capacity to frame these narratives. If they neglect to do so, the unilateral model will continue to expand, particularly in weak institutional frameworks such as those in North America.

Notes

1 The research for this article was financed by grants from the International Development Research Centre of Canada, the Social Sciences and Humanities Research Council of Canada and the Fonds québécois de recherche sur la société et la culture. We would like to thank the many trade unionists in Mexico who made this research possible and particularly Alejandro Rangel. We would also like to thank Carlos Gracia, Bodil Damgaard, Alejandro Espinosa and Marc-Antonin Hennebert-Faulkner for their contribution to the data collection.
2 It is estimated that the active labour force is growing by 1.5 per cent per year, or roughly 1.5 million new labour market entrants, and that only

half of these people manage to obtain employment in the formal economy (Cosio-Zavala, 2001).

3 It should be stressed that, prior to the election of Vicente Fox, the Institutional Revolutionary Party (PRI) was the party of government from the early 1930s to the year 2000. The PRI had always maintained very close ties with the official unions, notably the CTM. The official unions acted like a transmission belt for the PRI, which controlled the levers of state power, and they contributed greatly to the PRI's electoral hegemony (Middlebrook, 1995).

4 Generally, the sections of the CTM's regional amalgamated unions do not enjoy such autonomy. Union dues are managed at a more centralised level and the executive committee is replaced by delegates with less autonomy (Bayón, 1997; Middlebrook, 1995).

5 It should be noted that the agreement as a whole is renegotiated every two years, while pay is negotiated annually.

References

Almond, P., T. Edwards, T. Colling, A. Ferner, P. Gunningle, M. Müller-Camen, J. Quintanilla and H. Wächter (2005) 'Unravelling Home and Host Country Effects: An Investigation of the HR Policies of an American Multinational in Four European Countries', *Industrial Relations*, 44, 2: 276–306.

Arteaga, A. (2000) *Integración productiva y relaciones laborales en la industria automotriz en Mexico*. Tesis de Maestro. Mexico: Universidad Nacional Autonoma de Mexico.

Bayón, M.C. (1997) *El sindicalismo automotriz mexicano frente a un nuevo escenario: una perspectiva desde los liderazgos*. Mexico: Juan Pablos Editor.

Bélanger, J. and P.K. Edwards (2006) 'Towards a Political Economy Framework: TNCs as National and Global Players'. In *Multinationals and the Construction of Transnational Practices*, A. Ferner, J. Quintanilla and C. Sànchez-Runde (eds) London: Palgrave Macmillan, 24–52.

Bélanger, J., A. Giles and J.N. Grenier (2003) 'Patterns of Corporate Influence in the Host Country: A Study of ABB in Canada", *International Journal of Human Resource Management*, 14: 3, 469–85.

Bensusán, G. (2000) *El modelo mexicano de regulación laboral*. Mexico: Friedrich Ebert Stiftung.

Bensusán, G. (2006) 'Occasions de renouveau syndical au Mexique sous le premier gouvernement de transition', *Relations Industrielles*, 61, 4: 708–31.

Bensusán, G. and M.L. Cook (2003) 'Political Transition and Labor Revitalization in Mexico'. In *Labor Revitalization: Global Perspectives and New Initiatives*, D.B. Cornfield and H.J. McCammon (eds) *Research in the Sociology of Work*, 11: 229–67.

Carrillo, J. (2004) 'NAFTA: The Process of regional Integration of Motor Vehicle Production'. In *Cars, Carriers of Regionalism?* J. Carrillo, Y. Lung and R. van Tulder (eds). New York: Palgrave Macmillan, 104–20.

Carrillo, J. and R. Partida (eds) (2004) La Industria Maquiladora Mexicana. Tijuna: El Colegio de la Frontera Norte.

Cosio-Zavala, M.-E. (2001) 'La population mexicaine en 2000: évolutions et comportements nouveaux', *Problèmes d'Amérique Latine*, no. 40, 75–92.

CTM-COMPARMEX (1995) *Acuerdos por una nueva cultura Obrera*. Mexico: Semanario CTM, no. 2219.

de la Garza, E. (1998) 'Flexibilidad del trabajo y contratación colectiva en México', *Revista Mexicana de Sociología*, 60: 87–122.

de la Garza, E. (2003) 'Mexican Trade Unionism in the Face of Political Transition', in *Labor Revitalization: Global Perspectives and New Initiatives*, D.B. Cornfield and H.J. McCammon (eds). *Research in the Sociology of Work*, 11: 202–28.

de la O Martínez, M.E. (2001) 'Ciudad Juárez: un Polo de Crecimiento Maquilador', in *globalización, Trabajo y Maquilas: Las Nuevas y Viejas Fronteras en México*, M.E. de la O Martínez and C. Quintero Ramírez (eds) México: Friedrich Ebert Stiftung, 25–72.

Dombois, R. (1999) 'Tendencias en las transformaciones de la relaciones laborales en América Latina: Los Casos de Brasil, Colombia y México', in *Globalización y cambios en las relaciones industriales*, L. Pries and E. De La Garza (eds) Mexico: Friedrich Ebert Stiftung, 15–52.

Dufour, C. and Hege, A. (2002) *L'Europe syndicale au quotidien*. Bruxelles: P.I.E. Peter Lang.

Frost, A.C. (2001) 'Reconceptualizing Local Union Responses to Workplace Restructuring in North America'. *British Journal of Industrial Relations*, 39: 539–64.

Gereffi, G. (2003) 'Mexico's Industrial Development: Climbing Ahead or Falling Behind in the World Economy', in *Confronting Development: Assessing Mexico's Economic and Social Policy Challenges*, K.J. Middlebrook and E. Zepeda (eds) Stanford: Stanford University Press, 195–240.

Huxley, C. (2003) 'Local Union Responses to Continental Standardization of Production and Work in GM's North American Truck Assembly Plant', in *Multinational Companies and Global Human Resource Strategies*, W.N. Cook (eds) Westport, Quorum Books, 223–48.

Kristensen, P.H. and J. Zeitlin (2005) *Local Players in Global Games: The Strategic Constitution of a Multinational Corporation*. Oxford: Oxford University Press.

Lévesque, C. and G. Murray (2002) 'Local versus Global: Activating Local Union Power in the Global Economy', *Labor Studies Journal*, 27 (3): 39–65.

Lévesque, C. and G. Murray (2005) 'Union Involvement and Workplace Change: A Comparative Study of Local Unions in Canada and Mexico', *British Journal of Industrial Relations*, vol. 43: 3, 489–514.

Martin, G. and Beaumont, P. (1999) 'Co-ordination and control of human resource management in multinational firms: the case of CASHCO', *International Journal of Human Resource Management*, vol. 10, no. 1, 21–42.

Middlebrook, K.J. (1995) *The Paradox of Revolution: Labor, the State and authoritarianism in Mexico*. Baltimore: John Hopkins University Press.

Middlebrook, K.J. and E. Zepeda (2003) 'On the Political Economy of Mexican Development Policy', in *Confronting Development: Assessing Mexico's Economic and Social Policy Challenges*, K.J. Middlebrook and E. Zepeda (eds). Stanford: Stanford University Press, 3–54.

Montiel Hernández, Y. (2003) *Un Mondo de Coches, Nuevas Formas de Organización del Trabajo*. México: Ciesas.

Pries, L., G. Garcia and C. Gutierrez (2000) *Entre el corporativismo productivista y la participación de los trabajadores: globalización y relaciones industriales en la industria automotriz mexicana*. Mexico: Universidad Autónoma Metropolitana.

Pulignano, V. (2006) 'Patterns of integration in American multinational subsidiaries in Europe', in A. Ferner, J. Quintanilla and C. Sanchez-Runde (eds) Multinationals, Institutions and the Construction of Transnational Practices. London: Palgrave, 131–54.

Salas, C. and E. Zepeda (2003) 'Employment and Wages: Enduring the Costs of Liberalization and Economic Reform', in *Confronting Development: Assessing Mexico's Economic and Social Policy Challenges*, K.J. Middlebrook and E. Zepeda (eds) Stanford: Stanford University Press, 522–60.

Servin, F.H. (2002) 'El aumento de los salarios mínimos', *El Financiero*, 29 de enero, 14.

Tuman, J.P. (2003) *Reshaping the North American Automobile Industry: Restructuring, Corporatism, and Union democracy in Mexico*. New York: Continuum.

Index